THE HELMSLEY WALLE
COOK BOOK

Compiled, edited and introduced by

Elke Laver

Illustrated by

Sarah Balme
Bridget Gillespie
David Goodall
John Grove-Stephenson
Elizabeth Hawksworth
Anne Lang

THE HELMSLEY WALLED GARDEN
COOK BOOK

Published by Helmsley Walled Garden Limited

© Helmsley Walled Garden Limited 2004
www.helmsleywalledgarden.co.uk

ISBN No 0 9547090 0 4

Printed by Maxiprint/PDQ
Kettlestring Lane, Clifton Moor, York YO30 4XF
www.maxiprint.co.uk

ABOUT THE HELMSLEY WALLED GARDEN

The Helmsley Walled Garden lies close to the centre of Helmsley, directly below the Tudor wing of Helmsley Castle added to the thirteenth century castle towards the end of the sixteenth century. It has been part of the Duncombe estates for more than three hundred years. It was moved to its present protected site by the Duncombe family in 1756 after they had moved into the newly built Duncombe Park in 1713. Previously, the kitchen garden had been located to the south on the bank of the river Rye; it had been destroyed by a flood in 1754. The garden's original purpose was to provide the Duncombe family with a continuous supply of vegetables, fruit and flowers. In the late eighteenth or early nineteenth century glass houses were added. The present glass houses along the walls date from 1850, the current Orchid House from 1910. The Duncombe family employed nineteen gardeners at one time, the most famous being head gardener Michael Rochford (1819-83), an important figure in the history of glasshouses, who cultivated, lemon and orange trees together with pineapples and vines in the Garden. Named cultivars included 'Feversham's Pine' and 'Rochford's Grape'. In 1914 the Duncombe Estate stopped using the Garden and leased it to a market gardener. During World War II the garden was ploughed over as part of the Dig for Victory campaign. It lost many original features and in 1984 it was abandoned and fell into dereliction.

The restoration of the Garden was begun in 1994 as a personal crusade by the late Alison Ticehurst who leased the Garden from the Duncombe Estate. She believed in the healing power of gardening and wanted the Garden to become part of the life of the town of Helmsley and its citizens as a community resource. The response was immediate and her vision attracted and continues to attract many volunteers. The aim is to restore all structures within the garden to their original appearance, using local artisans where possible and historically appropriate materials. 1997 saw the appointment of the present Head Gardener, Paul Radcliffe, and the Assistant Manager, Lindsay Tait. In 1999 the Garden became a registered charity with Martin Constantine as its first chairman. The charity's purpose is the promotion of education and training, employment and horticultural therapy to help those with disabilities and special needs. After the tragically early death of Alison Ticehurst in 1999, her work was carried on by her friends and the restoration of the Garden has continued to make great progress. The Garden now conserves a wide range of plants – a burgeoning collection of orchids, a hundred northern varieties of apples and pears under the auspices of the Northern Fruit Group, and almost two hundred varieties of clematis as the site of the British Clematis Society's display garden. The restoration has been helped by grants from the Heritage Lottery Fund and other benefactors. In 2002 the restoration of the Orchid House was completed but major tasks remain. The Heritage Lottery Fund has awarded a grant of five hundred and five thousand pounds to rebuild the glass houses on the south wall including the historic Vineries and all the outbuildings. The Helmsley Walled Garden Trust has to raise ninety thousand pounds in matching-funds of which, at the time of writing, more than seventy thousand pounds has been found .

ABOUT THIS COOK BOOK

Yorkshire cookery is generally regarded as a bastion of traditional cooking. It has its own regional history going back to Roman times. Dishes such as curd tarts and nettle soup, now considered as typically Yorkshire, have Roman roots. After the links of the region to the Roman Empire were severed, monasteries and great houses again took up these culinary traditions. They cultivated herbs and vegetables the Romans had introduced in their gardens. Innovations in food preparation arrived slowly in Yorkshire. Recipes were handed down from mother to daughter, very often for food eaten at special occasions. They were used and refined over several generations. Both Yorkshire pudding and parkin have early origins. In the area around Helmsley and in North Yorkshire in general, traditional foods and their customary preparation still thrive. The farm lands, woods and streams of the region provide rich offerings of meats, game and fish as well as every kind of fruit and vegetable. Horticulture has been a preoccupation over centuries. The surviving walled gardens bear witness to that. Today, of all the hobbies gardening is the most prevalent. Home-baking, to a very high standard, is still widely practised. Yorkshire cooking has undergone in the last decades a gentle revolution, away from trencherman's food to a sophisticated use of traditional recipes and local ingredients. In this region of Yorkshire, surprisingly many inns and restaurants successfully marry tradition and originality. Many local families have recipe collections of their own.

This book cannot do full justice to local culinary talent in all its variety. It attempts nonetheless to give a reasonably representative cross section of contemporary cooking in the area. The recipes in the book have been generously provided by local people and businesses who care for both the excellence of local cuisine and the welfare of the Helmsley Walled Garden. They have passed on culinary secrets and let us have old family recipes. Some have also provided favourite recipes brought home from trips and holidays abroad. The contributors come from all walks of life and the recipes reflect that. They cover a wide range of different styles and degrees of difficulty. Like the Walled Garden itself, the cook book is a community project: All recipes have been volunteered. The same is true of the illustrations and the editing. It is the intention that the proceeds from the sale of this booklet will bolster the finances of the Garden Trust for recurring projects. Special thanks are due to all those who have contributed recipes – their names are listed opposite. Lady Feversham, Sir David Goodall, Lin Hawthorne and Paul Radcliffe, have been specially helpful, patiently making useful suggestions, reading the proofs and giving support in many ways, in addition to providing recipes. Sincere appreciation to Dr. Peter Ticehurst who kindly permitted the use of papers of the late Alison Ticehurst, and also to the artists who provided illustrations: Sarah Balme, Bridget Gillespie, Sir David Goodall, John Grove-Stephenson, Elizabeth Hawksworth and Anne Lang. A list of the illustrations is included on page vi. Particular gratitude is owed to the Local Heritage Initiative, a partnership between the Heritage Lottery Fund, Nationwide Building Society and the Countryside Agency, whose generosity has made the book's production possible as part of a wider Local Heritage Initiative project of the Helmsley Walled Garden.

CONTRIBUTORS

We gratefully acknowledge the generous contribution of recipes by friends of the Walled Garden and by members of the community, which has made this book possible. We list the contributors here in alphabetical order.

Ampleforth Abbey
The Appletree Country Inn, Marton
Sarah Balme, Gillamoor
The Black Swan, Helmsley
Audrey Bulmer, Keldholme
Neil and Dorothy Booth, Hovingham
Ian Carmichael, Grosmont
Dawn Carvey, Dalton-on-Tees
The Rev. Father Leo Chamberlain OSB, Ampleforth College
Anne Cobb, Sinnington
Lady Clarissa Collin, Pockley
Martin and Jane Constantine, Byland Abbey
The late Glory Duncombe, Helmsley
The Durham Ox, Crayke
Lorna Fawcett, Kirkbymoorside
Lady Feversham, Helmsley
The Fox and Hounds Country Inn, Sinnington
Bridget Gillespie, Beadlam
Sir David and Morwenna Goodall, Ampleforth
The Rev. Susan Greenwood, Helmsley
The Hare Inn, Scawton
Lin Hawthorne, Rievaulx
The Hon Simon Howard, Castle Howard
Mary Hughes, Keldholme

Pat Hughes, Helmsley
Hunters of Helmsley, Helmsley
Rosanna and Oliver James, Sleightholmedale
The Kings Head Hotel, Kirkbymoorside
Anne Lang, Hawnby
Elke Laver, Keldholme
Paul Radcliffe, Helmsley
Piers Paul Read, London
The Pheasant Hotel, Harome
Shallowdale House, Ampleforth
George Smith and Brian Withill, Heslington
Pat Speed, Helmsley
The Star Inn, Harome
The late Alison Ticehurst, Helmsley
Margery Turner, Helmsley
Martin Vander Weyer, Helmsley
Peter N. Walker, Ampleforth
The Walled Garden Café, Helmsley
John Warrack and Lucy Beckett, Rievaulx
Marguerite Weyer, Helmsley
The White Swan, Ampleforth
The Rev. David Wilbourne, Helmsley
The Wombwell Arms, Wass
Moira Wood, Helmsley
The Hon.Lady Worsley, Hovingham

ILLUSTRATIONS

Alison Ticehurst, Elizabeth Hawksworth
Ampleforth Abbey, Sir David Goodall
The Black Swan, Helmsley, Anne Lang
Byland Abbey, Sir David Goodall
Castle Howard, Sir David Goodall
Castle Howard, View from across the Lake, Sir David Goodall
Castle Howard, Temple of the Four Winds, Sir David Goodall
Castlegate, Helmsley, Anne Lang
Cover, Bridget Gillespie
Duncombe Park Garden Front, Sir David Goodal
Duncombe Park, Nelson Arch, Sir David Goodall
Duncome Park, Doric Temple, John Grove Stephenson
Duncombe Park, Ionic Temple, John Grove-Stephenson
The Hare Inn Scawton, Sir David Goodall
The Helmsley Walled Garden, Sir David Goodall
Hovingham Hall, Sir David Goodall
Lemons and Sugar, Sarah Balme
Lemons, Bridget Gillespie
Rievaulx Abbey, Sir David Goodall
The Star Inn, Harome, Sir David Goodall
The White Swan, Ampleforth, Sir David Goodall
Wombwell Arms, Wass, Sir David Goodall

CONTENTS

Starters are essential for a good festive meal, wetting the appetite for the serious matter of the main course, and clearly a field where the contributors to this book have invested culinary imagination and creativity. They have come up with mouth-watering proposals for a beginning full of flavours, often with an interesting twist.

20. VIII. 03   DUNCOMBE PARK

TURBOT IN FILO PASTRY WITH A SAFFRON SAUCE

SERVES 6

This is a recipe for a delicate and unusual starter from Lady Feversham of Duncombe Park.

Built for Sir Charles Duncombe, goldsmith and banker to Charles II, the house has been in the ownership of the family since 1713; but following the death of the second Earl at the Battle of the Somme, it was leased to a girls' preparatory school and remained in institutional use for nearly seventy years. In 1986, the present Lord and Lady Feversham decided to reclaim Duncombe Park as a family home and instigated a large-scale restoration project with the aim of opening the house and gardens for the enjoyment of a wider public.

Lady Feversham's interest in food was awakened by time spent in France, first as a child and later as a student. But she credits her mother-in-law, Glory Duncombe, who lived in the house overlooking the Walled Garden, with introducing her to the art of cookery. As well as writing and lecturing, Lady Feversham loves helping to preserve the architectural heritage of the house in its 35 acres of landscaped park land, described by Sacheverell Sitwell as a 'supreme masterpiece of the art of the landscape gardener'.

800g (1¾lb) turbot, skinned, boned
   and cut into small cubes

6 leaves of filo pastry

6 chives, blanched – or 6 long thin
   strips of leek, blanched

25g (1oz) butter, melted

2 tsp dill, finely chopped

salt and black pepper

For the saffron sauce:

350ml (12floz) good fish stock

250ml (9floz) dry white wine

225ml (8floz) Noilly Prat

300ml (11floz) double cream

several strands of saffron

50g (2oz) chilled butter

continued

Pat the cubes of turbot dry, season well with salt and pepper, and divide between the six sheets of filo pastry. Sprinkle with the chopped dill and draw up the corners of each sheet so that each little parcel looks like a money bag. Tie each carefully with either a blanched chive or a strip of blanched leek. Brush with melted butter and bake for 12 minutes in a preheated oven at 190°C/375°F/gas mark 5.

For the saffron sauce, bring the first four sauce ingredients to a rapid boil and reduce until 8 floz remain. Add cream and bring back to the boil. Reduce until the sauce coats the back of a spoon Add saffron and whisk in the butter. Strain and season.

Place the little turbot parcels on a warmed plate and spoon the saffron sauce around.

LADY CLARISSA'S SALMON MOUSSE

Lady Clarissa Collin, the only daughter of the 3rd and last Earl of Feversham, lives at Wytherstone House in Pockley in the North York Moors National Park, just a couple of miles north-east of Helmsley. The house is guarded by two sculpted foxes and surrounded by gardens created over the past thirty five years by Lady Clarissa. It is a large, ever expanding plantsman's paradise full of rare shrubs and perennials. Beech hedges divide the landscape into rooms of different character – a border of acid loving plants, a rock garden, a sunken garden, an aboretum and many more. There are greenhouses and cold frames full of interesting and unusual plants. A range of these plants can be bought from the nursery on open days; groups can visit by appointment .

275ml (½ pt) white sauce
½ tsp dry mustard
2tbsp wine vinegar
2 eggs separated
225g (8oz) cooked salmon
4 tbsp double cream
35-40g (1-1½oz) gelatine
3 tbsp water
salt and pepper
cucumber for garnish

Make up white sauce, add mustard, seasoning and vinegar, simmer for two minutes. Beat in egg yolks and cook for two more minutes. Remove from heat, add flaked salmon and cream. Dissolve gelatine in hot water, cool slightly and then stir in the salmon mixture. Leave until nearly set, then fold in the stiffly beaten egg whites. Pour into a bowl or greased mould and leave to set. Dip the base of the mould into hot water for a few seconds to loosen the mousse before turning it out. Garnish with cucumber.

LOBSTER HENDERSKELFE

SERVES 4

Castle Howard was built by Charles Howard, the third Earl of Carlisle, after a design of Sir John Vanbrugh on the site of the Old Castle of Henderskelfe which had been gutted by fire in 1693. Building work probably begun in 1699 but it took more than a hundred years before Castle Howard was completed. It is generally considered to be the finest private residence in Yorkshire, famous not only for its architecture but for its art collections and the magnificent gardens which surround it. In 2002, the Hon. Simon Howard invited archaeologists to dig for the remains of the lost village of Henderskelfe razed to the ground by the third Earl. He has given us this recipe, named after the site of Castle Howard. The dish is a good opening for a festive meal.

Meat of a large lobster, boiled (yield usually 500g/1lb)
75g (2½oz) butter
1 clove garlic crushed
2 shallots finely chopped
pinch of thyme
pinch of rosemary
1 dessertspoon chives
275 ml (½pt) double cream
salt and freshly ground pepper to taste

Cook shallots and garlic in the melted butter until soft but without letting them brown. Add lobster and cream. Allow to cook gently through until very hot, adding herbs and seasoning. Garnish with coral and chives.

POTTED CRAB

SERVES 4

Martin Constantine, the first Chairman of the Walled Garden Board and its present Secretary, had given Alison Ticehurst a helping hand at an early stage, masterminding ways of making the Garden administratively and financially viable. As she writes in her papers: he "…had answered an appeal for help…and had spent much time with me and my solicitor trying to find our way through to charitable status and a company."

He and his wife Jane are great gardeners in their own right. Their house, surrounded by a beautifully landscaped garden, overlooks the ruins of Byland Abbey. Jane who has a great interest in cookery has provided this recipe.

225g (8oz) crabmeat
75g (3oz) butter
3 egg yolks
2 tbsp cream
1 tbsp sherry or brandy
salt and pepper
cayenne
1 tbsp parmesan cheese, grated

Put the crabmeat, white and brown mixed, into a pan with the butter, egg yolks, cream and sherry or brandy. Stir over a low heat till well blended and thick. Season lightly with salt, pepper, cayenne and a tablespoon of parmesan cheese. Pack into individual cocotte dishes and chill.

SMOKED HADDOCK MOUSSE

SERVES 6

The watercolorist Audrey Bulmer lives with her husband John in the ancient Duna Cottage on the river Dove in Keldholme. She is a member of the North Riding Arts Group of painters and exhibits mostly in Ryedale as well as undertaking commissions for flower still-lifes and house exteriors. She is an avid gardener and an imaginative cook. She has given us this recipe.

500g (1lb) smoked haddock fillet
1 slice of onion
a few parsley stalks
15g (½oz) powdered gelatine
juice of ½ lemon
575ml (1pt) water
pepper, freshly milled
275ml (½pt) double cream
2 eggs, hard boiled and sliced
a few cucumber slices

Cut the smoked haddock into small pieces; put them into a pan with the onion and parsley stalks and water; bring to a boil and cook, covered gently, for 10 minutes. Transfer the fish to a plate and, when cool enough to handle, flake it, discarding skin and bones. Strain 275ml/ ½ pint of the cooking liquid into the rinsed-out pan, sprinkle the gelatine in and leave to soak for 5 minutes. Put pan back on low heat and stir until the gelatine has dissolved. **Do not allow to boil.** Pour the fish liquid into a medium sized bowl and leave to cool. When the mixture begins to thicken, stir in the flaked haddock, lemon juice and pepper. Whip the cream and fold in. Spoon the mousse into a serving dish or ramekins. Decorate with slices of hard boiled egg and with cucumber slices. Serve with thinly sliced brown bread and butter.

SMOKED MACKEREL PÂTÉ

SERVES 4

Moira Wood is an artist who paints with a needle assembling collages of radiant colours from pieces of fabric. Her other great interest is gardening. She serves on the committee of the Helmsley Garden Club and was a volunteer who started, with Alison Ticehurst, to revive the Walled Garden. For her, weeding has become a form of therapy. She has let us have this practical recipe.

2 smoked mackerel, skinned and boned
150g (6oz) cream cheese
75g (3oz) fresh or tinned pineapple, chopped
4 gherkins, finely chopped
freshly ground pepper
dash of tabasco

Skin the mackerel and remove the bones. Blend all the ingredients together. Salt is not necessary. Serve the pâté in ramekins, or shape portions with an ice cream scoop and surround them with a few mixed salad leaves. Garnish with a gherkin fan or herbs. Crunchy brown bread, butter and lemon are suitable accompaniments. The whole process of assembling, blending and serving need take no longer than ten minutes.

Instead of mackerel kippers may be used but are more difficult to de-bone. The combination of pineapple with the smoked fish complements their strong flavour.

YORKSHIRE PUDDINGS AND POOR MAN'S SALAD

SERVES 6-8

The Durham Ox in the beautiful village of Crayke on the southern edge of the North York Moors carries its name because the village, despite its geographical position, used to belong to the County Palatine of Durham. For a time, the body of St Cuthbert was hidden from Danish invaders at Crayke. It only became part of the North Riding in the middle of the nineteenth century. The old inn specialises in traditional English food and is famous for its Sunday lunches. A classical menu would consist of Yorkshire Puddings and Poor Man's Salad as a first course, followed by Roast Rib of Beef and finished with Sticky Toffee Pudding. Yorkshire pudding served in the great tradition is accompanied by gravy and salad. It is held that, by filling up on pudding, people would consume less meat.

For the Yorkshire puddings:
4 good tbsp plain flour
pinch of salt
2 large eggs
milk
oil, dripping or goose fat

For the Poor Man's Salad:
1 head of lettuce, chopped up
a few spring onions, chopped
handful of mint leaves, chopped
2 tbsp sugar
vinegar

The Inn's chef, Jason Plevey, would normally use about 22 eggs for his Yorkshires. This is a scaled down version. In a roomy bowl, put 4 good tablespoons of plain flour and a pinch of salt. Make a well in the middle and crack in two large eggs. With a firm hand and a wooden spoon, gradually draw the flour into the eggs; add milk, a little at a time, until a smooth – no lumps! – batter is obtained. The batter should be the consistency of pouring cream. Leave to stand, not in the fridge but in a cool spot in the kitchen.

The tin must be greased well. Oil, dripping or, the ultimate, goose fat can be used but the bottom of the tin must be well-covered. After the beef for the Sunday roast is taken out of the oven and set to rest, turn up the oven heat to 200-220°C/400-425°F/gas mark 6-7 and heat the tin until smoking. Just before you open the oven door, add a splash of cold tap water to the batter and beat well. Pour the batter quickly into the tin and close the door. 10 minutes or so later, you will have Yorkshire puddings. To summarise the Inn's secrets: a firm hand, a splash of tap water, a hot oven – and never wash the tin!

For the salad, chop up a lettuce – please not an iceberg! – a few spring onions and a handful of mint. Just before serving, dress with a sprinkle of sugar and some vinegar. In the old days, the outside leaves were picked from the growing lettuce and green onion tops gleaned from the garden.

HAM HOCK TERRINE WITH APPLE CHUTNEY

SERVES 8-10

Melanie Thornton and TJ Drew took over the reins at the Appletree Country Inn in Marton in March 2001 and have made it in the short time span since an exciting eating place. 'Creative food' and 'friendly service' are their terms of reference, earning them the Customer Service Pub of the Year 2002 award, among many others. Here is a recipe for an easy starter that tastes great.

2 large ham shanks
1 tbsp grainy mustard
handful of chopped parsley
pepper
1 large carrot, cut into pieces
   (optional)
1 large onion, coarsely chopped
   (optional)
2 cloves of garlic, crushed (optional)
2 celery stalks, coarsely chopped
   (optional)
sprig of thyme (optional)
a few bay leaves (optional)
small orange sliced (optional) OR
2-3 sprigs of lavender (optional)

For the chutney:
1½ kilo (3½lb) cooking apples,
   peeled, cored and roughly
   chopped
650g (1½lb) onions, chopped
300g (11oz) raisins
2 lemons, thinly sliced and slices cut
   in half
½ litre cider vinegar
400g (14oz) dark sugar
1 tbsp salt
1 tbsp ground ginger
1 tbsp ground cinnamon
1 tsp turmeric

Cover the ham shanks with water and boil for 2-3 hours until tender. For extra flavour, add carrot, onion, garlic, thyme, bay leaves and celery to the pot. Adding orange to the cooking liquid will give a citrus zing, while lavender will give the dish a delicate perfumed touch. Do not boil dry. When hams are cooked take them out of the liquid to cool. Keep the cooking liquid..

Now the messy bit: When the hams are cool enough to handle, remove all excess fat and pick the meat from the bones into a large bowl. Then add mustard and parsley and season with pepper only. Strain a little of the cooking liquid into the mixture until it is just short of being sloppy. Mix well.

Place this mixture into moulds such as terrines or bread tins lined with cling film. Cover and allow to set in the refrigerator over night. To serve, turn out of the container and slice onto a bed of lettuce with a dollop of chutney or pineapple relish, or whatever you fancy. The terrine can also be served with a poached egg for a slightly more unusual ham and egg variation.

For the apple chutney, place the apples in a heavy-bottomed pan with the onions, raisins and lemon slices. Add the vinegar and bring to the boil, then simmer until the apples are just softening. This takes about 10-20 minutes. Then add the sugar, gently stirring until it is dissolved. Simmer until the mixture thickens. Finally, add the salt and spices. Spoon into sterilised jars and seal. After one month the chutney will be ready to use. This simple recipe can be altered to make other variations, such as ginger and apple chutney by doubling the ginger content, or adding chilli for that extra spicy flavour. This goes well with pork dishes or with cheese.

POTTED CHICKEN LIVER

SERVES 4-6

This recipe for a very rich pâté also comes from Jane Constantine of Byland Abbey.

100g (3½oz) butter
1 small onion, very finely chopped
1 or 2 cloves of garlic, crushed
350g (12oz) chicken livers
2 tbsp brandy
2 tbsp madeira or sherry
2 tbsp wine vinegar
black pepper, freshly ground
pinch of powdered allspice
salt to taste

Melt 40g/1½oz of the butter and cook the chopped onion and the crushed garlic in it until soft. Add chicken livers and cook gently for 5 minutes, turning them over now and again. Take the onion and livers out. Pour into the pan 2 tablespoons of brandy and 2 tablespoons of madeira or sherry. Simmer, scraping up all the bits and juices from the pan. Put the pan juices into a blender or mincer together with the roughly chopped chicken livers and 60g/2oz of softened butter, 2 tablespoons wine vinegar, some freshly ground black pepper, a pinch of powdered allspice and salt to taste. Reduce the mixture to a purée, turn into an earthenware dish, cover and chill. This rich pâté, like all pâtés, is best kept for a few days before eating.

NELSON ARCH

ROASTED PEPPERS

SERVES 6

Lady Feversham has given us this recipe.

3 sweet red peppers
3 tomatoes
6 anchovies
12 basil leaves
salt and pepper
2-3tbsp olive oil
6 slices of cheese, preferably mozzarella

Cut the red peppers in half and de-seed. In each half place, half a tomato, an anchovy and two basil leaves. Season well, sprinkle with olive oil and place a slice of cheese on top. Roast in a hot oven (220°C/425°F/gas mark7) for 20 minutes
.

COURGETTE FLOWERS IN BATTER

SERVES 1

Pat Hughes has been a volunteer at the Walled Garden for eight years, from the very start of the project. She has been helping with many tasks in the Garden. Now she helps to look after the Orchid House. She has learned how to prune roses, makes Christmas wreaths and enjoys picking fruit and vegetables. She assists with the organisation of art exhibitions there. Her talents as an imaginative cook have been deployed for social events at the Garden. She has let us have this recipe.

**3 to 4 male courgette flowers per person
4 tbsp white flour
1 tsp bicarbonate of soda
100ml (3½floz) water
juice of 1 lemon
salt and pepper
1 tbsp olive oil**

Male courgette flowers are the ones on long stalks without an attached courgette. If you can't get any, you could use tiny whole courgettes with the flower still attached from your own garden. Otherwise, use large courgettes cut into thin slices, half a centimetre (¼") thick. Wash the flowers well and let them dry.

For the batter, put flour and bicarbonate of soda into a bowl. Whisk in the water to make a smooth batter and stir in lemon juice and seasoning.

Heat the oil in a shallow pan. Dip the flowers into the batter, shaking off the excess, and fry until golden underneath, pressing lightly down on each flower with a fish slice to flatten. Turn over and repeat. This flattening produces a crispy finish. Drain on kitchen paper and serve immediately with a good quality mayonnaise into which a crushed clove of garlic has been stirred.

THE
HELMSLEY
WALLED GARDEN

CUCUMBER MOUSSE WITH DILL FLAGEOLETS

SERVES 4-6

Lin Hawthorne is a horticulturist, writer and editor of gardening books. Among many other things, she is an authority on roses and rhododendrons and contributes a monthly column to the RHS Journal The Garden. A consultant at the Helmsley Walled Garden, she compiled the conservation plan and co-ordinated the application that won an award of five hundred and five thousand pounds from the Heritage Lottery to restore the greenhouses.

For the cucumber mousse:
½ cucumber
275ml (½pt) whipping cream
225g (½lb) cream cheese
225g (½lb) cottage cheese
tarragon or other herb vinegar
good handful of fresh chives, parsley,
    spring onions, chopped
1 tbsp agar-agar or gelatine
salt and coarse ground pepper to
    taste

For the dill flageolets:
175g (6oz) flageolet beans, cooked –
    or from a tin
fresh dill or tarragon
mayonnaise, preferably home made

1 or 2 slices smoked salmon per
    person

For the cucumber mousse, peel and dice the cucumber. Mix with one heaped tablespoon of salt and three tablespoons of tarragon vinegar. Stand for 2-3 minutes, drain into a colander and press with a plate; leave for an hour, then rinse in cold fresh water and pat completely dry in clean cloth. Dissolve agar-agar or gelatine in hot water and whisk in the whipping cream. When smooth and thick, blend in cream cheese and cottage cheese. Stir in cucumber, black pepper and herbs. Pour into an oiled mould and leave to set in the fridge. Serve with crusty bread, salmon, green salad and dill flageolets. Makes an excellent starter or a light summer lunch.

For the dill flageolets, chop dill coarsely, mix in the mayonnaise and fold the flageolets into the mix. Also works well with tarragon.

PASTA WITH BLACK CABBAGE SAUCE

SERVES 4

Rosanna and Oliver James live in Sleightholmedale Lodge built in 1889 and given, in 1904, by the then Lord Feversham to his youngest daughter in whose family it remains. Magnificent hanging gardens run down a steep hillside from the house towards the Hodge Beck. Oliver James has a keen interest in his vegetable garden. It is his aim to be able to produce a home-grown salad every day of the year. He grows many varieties of chicory with red, green or marbled red and green leaves, which can survive frost, as well as other rare vegetables including the Tuscan black cabbage, cavalo nero *(Seeds available from The Organic Gardening Catalogue Tel 01932 253666). Black cabbage is in fact dark green and upright in growth. It is the essential ingredient in this favourite starter of theirs during the winter.*

200g (7oz) tagliatelle or other pasta
500g (1lb) black cabbage
50g (2oz) freshly grated parmesan
4 tbsp olive oil
1 small head of garlic
salt and pepper

Remove the stalks from the cabbage and boil it with two cloves of garlic for a few minutes. Drain well. Blend together with the rest of the garlic, olive oil and salt and pepper to a dark green purée. Cook the pasta in boiling salted water, drain and fold into the sauce. Serve with parmesan.

BROAD BEANS AND SMOKED HAM

SERVES 4

In summer time, Rosanna James serves this starter:

400g (14oz) garden-fresh small broad beans
200g (7oz) thinly sliced pancetta or good smoked bacon
1 tbsp finely chopped chives and/or
1 tbsp parsley, finely chopped

Cook tiny broad beans in boiling water for about two minutes. Drain well. Cut pancetta or smoked bacon into matchsticks, fry briefly and add to the beans. Serve warm sprinkled with finely chopped chives and parsley.

SWEET LETTUCE AND ONIONS

SERVES 4

The Minister of the Helmsley Methodist Church, the Rev. Susan Greenwood, has provided this light appetiser to be served before the Sunday roast.

1 head of lettuce, cut into small strips
6 salad onions, finely chopped
2 sprigs of mint, finely chopped
2 tbsp malt vinegar
50g (2oz) sugar

Mix all the ingredients and serve fresh.

PEARS WITH YORKSHIRE BLUE

SERVES 4

Pears and blue cheese marry well and make an easy starter.

8 pear halves, peeled, cored and poached in wine OR preserved pears
4 walnuts, shelled and chopped
125g (4oz) blue cheese, crumbled
3 handfuls of mixed salad leaves such as lettuce, rocket or watercress
vinaigrette

Arrange the pear halves on top of the salad leaves on individual plates. Sprinkle with walnuts and blue cheese. Just before serving drizzle vinaigrette over the pears

Soups can stand at the beginning of a meal but they can also be a meal in themselves as lunch or supper. There are refreshing summer and heart-warming winter soups. There is nothing better than a good soup after a hard day's work. Here is a good cross-section of what is cooking in the soup pot in and around Helmsley.

Ampleforth Abbey
暮 4.7.03

APPLE AND CHESTNUT SOUP

SERVES 6

The Benedictine community at Ampleforth celebrated its bicentennial there in 2002. It is best known for the public school attached to the Abbey. In horticultural circles, Ampleforth is well known for its collection of Northern apple varieties. According to monastic tradition, the Ampleforth orchard was first planted by Abbot Smith about a hundred years ago. In 1982, the Abbey published a book of recipes, "Cooking Apples", from which, with kind permission, the following recipes are taken.

500g (1lb) chestnuts in their shells (or preserved or deep frozen chestnuts)
1 stick celery
2 large dessert apples (Cox or Reinette) peeled, cored and sliced
50g (2oz) butter
1½ litres (3pts) light stock or water
125ml (4floz) single cream
salt and pepper

Make a cross-incision on the chestnuts and boil them for about twenty minutes. Shell them and cook them, with the chopped celery, in half of the stock for about twenty minutes or until the nuts are quite soft.

Meanwhile simmer the apple slices in the butter with a little salt and pepper. When both chestnuts and apples are soft, liquidise together in a blender and dilute to soup consistency. Adjust seasoning. Just before serving add the cream and stir. Serve with fried croutons.

CHILLED CUCUMBER AND APPLE SOUP

SERVES 6

This is another recipe from the Ampleforth Apple Cook Book.

2 large cucumbers, peeled
500g (1lb) cooking apples, peeled cored and sliced
1 lemon
1small clove of garlic, crushed
1 glass dry white wine
salt and pepper
125-200ml (4-7floz) sour cream or natural yoghurt
2-3 tbsp dill or fennel, finely chopped

Cook the apple slices gently in very little water with the juice and the grated rind of the lemon. Push them through a sieve or the medium disc of a Mouli-légumes; the purée should not be too smooth.

Put the apple purée into a large bowl and grate in the peeled cucumbers, using all the liquid, removing any large seeds. Sprinkle the mixture with sea salt and leave for at least two hours.

Add crushed garlic and wine, stir well and check the seasoning. Dilute if necessary. Sprinkle with chopped dill or fennel . Chill well and serve topped with a swirl of sour cream or a spoonful of yoghurt in each bowl.

ICED COURGETTE AND ROAST GARLIC SOUP

SERVES 6

John Warrack and Lucy Beckett are a married couple who have lived in Rievaulx since 1972. John is a former Oxford don and the author of a number of books on music; he is also President of the Ryedale Festival. Lucy was formerly Head of English at Ampleforth College; her books include volumes of poetry and criticism, and a novel, 'The Time Before You Die', set partly in Ryedale. Their garden has in it a beck that flows into the Rye, and the first and largest of three mill ponds made by the monks of Rievaulx Abbey in the middle ages to enable the beck to power the abbey mill. John grows a wide variety of fruit and vegetables; both of them cook; and Lucy makes a good deal of jam and chutney for the winter.

This recipe provided by them makes a lovely cold soup in summer when courgettes are plentiful and the garlic is strong. If you can lay your hands on smoked garlic – which is fairly common in France -, this adds a particularly delicious tang to the flavour. Though small courgettes are best for the purpose, slightly larger ones can be used with little loss of flavour. If you grow your own, you will be familiar with the phenomenon that one courgette can swell mysteriously overnight despite your careful searches the day before.

1 kilo (2lb) courgettes, thinly sliced
6-7 tbsp good olive oil
1500ml (3pt) light chicken stock
2 large garlic bulbs
salt and pepper
6 tbsp double cream
3 tbsp chives, chopped (optional)

Put the garlic bulbs to roast in a medium oven for about half an hour – if you have an Aga, the bottom right oven is ideal. Stew the thinly sliced courgettes in the oil, with the lid on the pan, until they are soft. Add the hot stock and simmer for about half an hour. Remove the flesh from the cloves of the garlic bulb with a sharp knife. Pour the whole mixture into a blender in instalments and then, when smooth, into a large bowl. Put in a refrigerator until thoroughly chilled. Season with salt and pepper. On serving, stir a little cream into each bowl and, if you like, chop in a few chives.

CUCUMBER AND YOGHURT SOUP

SERVES 4

The Helmsley Garden Club was founded in 2001. It is affiliated with the Walled Garden where many of its meetings take place. Marguerite Weyer, who has supported the Garden as a volunteer, is the Club's Chairman. She has let us have this recipe.

1 medium cucumber, peeled and de-seeded
500ml (2 cups) natural yoghurt
125g (½ cup) raisins, soaked in water
½ tsp salt
1 tbsp fresh dill, chopped
1 tbsp fresh mint or parsley, chopped

Peel and de-seed the cucumber; grate coarsely, Whisk the yoghurt in a deep bowl. Then add grated cucumber, drained raisins and all other ingredients. Refrigerate for at least two hours Check seasoning before serving. If too thick, add skim milk

CREAM OF FENNEL AND WATERCRESS SOUP

SERVES 4

Shallowdale House is a small guesthouse in the West End of Ampleforth surrounded by a large natural hillside garden overlooking the Howardian Hills. It offers impeccable accommodation and dinners cooked freshly of local produce – for residents only. The quality of the food is such that one of its regulars described it as Ampleforth's best kept secret. Since it is has recently been short listed for an 'England for Excellence Award', this may no longer be so . . .

50g (2oz) unsalted butter
1 onion chopped
2 large heads of fennel, chopped
100ml (4½floz) dry white wine
1 tsp fennel seeds
500ml (18floz) chicken stock
2 bunches fresh watercress
handful spinach leaves
150ml (¼pt) double cream
salt and pepper

Melt the butter and slowly sweat the fennel and onion in it, covered, until soft, stirring from to time Add the white wine and fennel seeds and simmer uncovered for three or four minutes. Add the chicken stock and cover, simmering for a further twenty minutes.

Meanwhile place the watercress in a pan of boiling water and boil for four minutes. Add the spinach and boil for one more minute. Drain immediately and refresh in cold water. Drain and allow to cool.

When the contents of the fennel pan are ready, place in a blender with the watercress and spinach. Blend until smooth. Sieve into a clean pan, add the cream and reheat gently without boiling. Season to taste

MEDITERRANEAN VEGETABLE SOUP WITH AIOLI

SERVES 10

The Kings Head Hotel in Kirkbymoorside can look back on a long history as an inn. Local tradition has it that George Villiers, the second Duke of Buckingham, died there in 1687 after he fell suddenly ill while hunting. After his death his extensive estates were sold by his trustees to Charles Duncombe who built Duncombe Park.

The former Chef Paul Sutton, a Yorkshireman, who has worked previously in a number of famous hotels and restaurants, let us have this recipe. His emphasis is on good quality food from local producers.

750g (1½lb) fresh plum tomatoes, chopped
2 red peppers, chopped
6 cloves of garlic, chopped
100ml (3½floz) olive oil
1 aubergine, chopped
2 courgettes chopped 2 red onions chopped
1 whole fennel, chopped
500g (1lb) sweet potatoes
4 sprigs of fresh thyme
50g (2oz) fresh coriander, coarsely chopped
50g (2oz) tomato paste
2½ litres (4½pts) water 2 bay leaves
salt and pepper to taste

For the aioli:
125g (4oz) mayonnaise
½ tsp turmeric
½ clove of garlic, finely chopped

Chop tomatoes, peppers and garlic together and roast in the oven for about twenty minutes. Then, heat olive oil in a pan and cook the potatoes, onions and fennel with bay leaves and sprigs of thyme for about ten to twelve minutes. Add courgettes, aubergine and tomato paste and cook for another three minutes. Then add the roasted tomatoes, peppers and garlic to the mixture, stir for two minutes and pour the water on it. Let the soup boil for about ten to twenty minutes. Simmer for ten further minutes. Take off the heat, remove bay leaves and sprigs of thyme and add the fresh coriander. Blend until fairly smooth. Season to taste.

For the aioli, mix mayonnaise, turmeric and ½ clove of finely chopped garlic Serve the soup with a small dollop of aioli on top.

ROASTED PEPPER AND TOMATO SOUP

SERVES 8

This soup is much easier to prepare than the previous one. Nonetheless it makes a good beginning for a meal, full of flavour. The recipe has been contributed by the delicatessen Hunters of Helmsley, who run an emporium full of delicacies for the discerning gourmet in the Market Place in Helmsley.

8 red, orange and yellow peppers
8 large tomatoes
4 cloves garlic crushed
handful of fresh basil, chopped
salt and pepper
pinch of sugar
4-5 tbsp olive oil
1½ litre (3pts) vegetable stock

Preheat the oven to 200°C (400°F). Cut the peppers in half and remove the seeds. Remove tomato stems and cut in half. Arrange tomatoes and peppers together with crushed garlic and chopped on a baking tray. Season with salt and pepper adding a pinch of sugar. Drizzle with olive oil and roast for twenty to thirty minutes in the oven.

Remove from the oven and put the vegetables into a sauce pan. Add the stock and bring to the boil. Liquidise and adjust seasoning.

POTATO AND LEEK SOUP

SERVES 6

Mary Hughes lives with her husband Brian in a cottage opposite the site of Keldholme Priory, There is little left of the medieval convent built by Robert de Stuttville in the twelfth century, just a few foundations and ancient burial slabs in a wall. But there is still a small, pretty village nestled around the site. Mary and Brian have created a lovely garden around their home and Mary has a knack for good cooking. This is one of her recipes.

4 large leeks, trimmed and washed thoroughly, cut into rings
2 medium potatoes, peeled and chopped
1 medium onion, chopped
50g (2oz) butter
750ml (1½ pt) chicken stock
250ml (½ pt) milk
salt and pepper
fresh chives, chopped

Melt the butter in a large sauce pan. Add leeks potatoes and onion. Stir until well coated with butter. Season with salt and pepper. Cover and sweat the vegetables over a low heat for fifteen minutes. Add stock and milk. Simmer for twenty minutes.

Cool slightly, liquidise to a purée and return to the pan. Adjust seasoning and sprinkle with chives before serving.

CREAMY CARROT AND ORANGE SOUP

SERVES 6-8

Lorna Fawcett is a garden designer and a founding member of the Helmsley Garden Club. Her own garden at Springwood shows how a quarry can be transformed. Here is one of her recipes.

25g (1oz) butter
1 large onion, coarsely chopped
1 kilo (2lb) carrots, thickly sliced
1½ litres (2½ pt) chicken or vegetable stock
grated zest of ½ orange
275ml (½pt) orange juice, ideally freshly squeezed
salt and black pepper
275ml (½pt) crème fraîche
handful of chives, snipped

Melt the butter in a large sauce pan, add the onion and cook gently for a few minutes until soft but not coloured. Add the carrots, cover and continue cooking for 10 minutes, stirring occasionally. Then add the stock and bring to the boil. Cover and simmer for 30 minutes. Purée in a food processor or blender until smooth. Return the soup to the rinsed-out pan, add salt and pepper to taste. Stir in the crème fraîche and gently reheat the soup. Stir in half of the snipped chives and sprinkle the soup with the rest just before serving.

GEORGETTE SOUP

SERVES 6

This vegetable soup takes its name from its texture – like that of the fabric georgette. Another recipe from Mary Hughes.

250g (½lb) ripe tomatoes
1 small head of celery, finely sliced
2 leeks or 1 onion, finely sliced
250g (½lb) carrot, finely sliced
25g (1oz) butter
25g (1oz) flour
1 litre (2pt) water
bay leaf
pinch of sugar
pinch of nutmeg or mace
1 tsp arrowroot (if necessary)
150ml (½pt) single cream
handful of chopped parsley or chives.

Peel and seed tomatoes, strain the pulp and reserve the juice. Place onion, celery and carrots in a pan with the butter to sweat; stir in flour. Add tomatoes, tomato juice, water, sugar, bay leaf, spice and seasoning. Bring to a boil while stirring and then simmer for 30 minutes. Sieve and return to the pan to reheat; if required, thicken with arrowroot (blended with a little water). Adjust seasoning to taste.

Boil soup for 1 minute, take off the heat and stir in the cream. Garnish with chopped parsley or chives.

NETTLE AND PEA SOUP

SERVES 4

The nettle still plays a role in Yorkshire folk medicine. The use of nettles in cooking and medicine was probably introduced by the Romans who brought with them a highly varied and balanced diet using wild plants like nettles and corn salad as well as new herbs like fennel and sage. Nettle soup is an old stand-by in Yorkshire. This new version makes a nice spring soup.

large bunch of spring nettles, washed and blanched
50-80g (2-3oz) butter
1 small onion, finely chopped
2 tbsp flour
300ml (11floz) chicken or vegetable stock
300ml (11floz) white wine
200g (7oz) fresh garden peas or frozen petits pois
50ml (2floz) sour cream

Purée the blanched nettles. Heat the butter in a casserole. Add the chopped onion and cook until softened. Stir in the flour and let it brown gently. Add stock and wine bit by bit while stirring. Now add the nettle purée and bring to a boil. After a few minutes add the peas and cook until they are *al dente*. Season with salt and pepper. Serve with a dollop of sour cream.

SALMON AND SPINACH SOUP

SERVES 4

A very practical soup when you have salmon leftovers

800ml (1½pt) fish stock, strained
200g (7oz) poached or roasted salmon, flaked
200-250g (7-9oz) fresh young spinach leaves
1-2 sprigs of dill or fennel fronds, finely chopped
50ml (2floz) dry sherry
salt and pepper

Heat the salmon pieces in the fish stock. Season with herbs, sherry, salt and pepper. Bring to a rolling boil and poach the spinach leaves shortly in the soup. Serve immediately.

JERUSALEM ARTICHOKE SOUP

SERVES 4

*The Jerusalem artichoke is not an artichoke, nor has it anything to do with Jerusalem.
It takes its name from girasole, the sunflower. It is a Peruvian sunflower, which was first
introduced into Europe in the seventeenth century. Its knobbly tubers make a comforting
soup, traditionally called 'Palestine soup'. Here is a simplified version. We call it
Walled Garden Soup', because, in autumn, the Garden is an excellent source of supply.
If one peels the tubers, the result is a beautifully white soup. It is much less labour-intensive
to thoroughly scrub the tubers before boiling and blending them; certainly at least as healthy,
but less appealing to the eye.*

1000g (2lb) Jerusalem artichokes
1-2 tbsp lemon juice or vinegar
600-800ml (1-1½pt) chicken or vegetable stock
2 tbsp fresh tarragon, chopped, or 1 tbsp dried tarragon
200g (7oz) Greek yoghurt
salt and pepper

Wash and peel the Jerusalem artichokes. Put them into a bowl of acidulated
water to prevent discoloration. Remove from the water and cut into large chunks.
Cover with chicken or vegetable stock and boil until tender. Purée artichokes
with the liquid, return to the heat, stir in the Greek yoghurt and add tarragon.
Adjust seasoning.

PHEASANT AND MUSHROOM SOUP

SERVES 6-8

Margery Turner has worked as a volunteer at the Walled Garden right from the beginning of its restoration. She is a member of the Board of Trustees and of the Helmsley Garden Club Committee. This is her recipe.

For the stock:
1 pheasant – any fat cut off
2 onions, cut in half with skins on
2 carrots
2 sticks of celery
4-6 cloves
1 tsp salt
4 black pepper corns

For the soup:
2 tbsp olive oil
2 onions, skinned and chopped
100g (4oz) Basmati rice
750g (1½lb) mushrooms, chopped small
1100ml (2pts) pheasant stock
pheasant meat, cooked and chopped
150ml (½pt) madeira or sherry
salt and pepper to taste

Make the stock by putting the washed pheasant together with the vegetables, cloves, salt and pepper corns into a casserole and cover with 3 pints of cold water. Bring slowly to a simmer. Cover with the lid and continue simmering for 2 hours. Let it cool. Take the pheasant out and cut the meat into small pieces. Strain the stock.

To make the soup, heat the oil and add the chopped onions. Cook for several minutes; then add the rice and cook for 2 more minutes while stirring. Then add the chopped mushrooms and the stock. Simmer gently for 45 minutes, stirring occasionally. Add the pheasant meat and madeira or sherry 10 minutes before serving. Check seasoning.

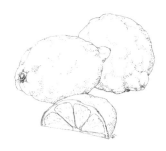

Salads like soups are of a hybrid nature: they can be the beginning of a meal, the accompaniment of a main course or a meal in themselves. On a hot summer's day there is nothing nicer than a salad meal in the garden, freshly made and bursting with flavour.

PAUL'S FRAGRANT HERB AND FLOWER SALAD

SERVES 4

Paul Radcliffe joined the Walled Garden as head gardener and garden manager in 1997. Since 1914 there had been no head gardener and the place had become derelict. Together with Alison Ticehurst and a growing number of volunteers he has been working at the revival of the garden. His efforts and his long hours of work have contributed greatly to the good shape the garden is in today. The ghost of Michael Rochford, the most famous head gardener at Duncombe Park, who became an authority on glass houses and pineapple growing and had a vine named after him, must be pleased to see what Paul has been able to achieve.

2 tomatoes sliced
½ cucumber thinly sliced
a few lettuce leaves torn
3 generous handfuls of fragrant garden-fresh herbs such as spear mint, ginger mint, Moroccan mint, coriander, flat-leafed parsley, dill, chervil, basil, lovage, fennel, oregano, chives, water cress, mustard cress, spinach, Swiss chard, nasturtium leaves, purslane.
1 small handful of flowers such as rose petals, nasturtiums, violas, borage flowers, pot marigold petals, day lilies, sweet pea or bean flowers, lavender, mint and elderberry flowers.
50 ml (3-4tbsp) vinaigrette (see recipe below)

Combine tomatoes, cucumber slices and lettuce with freshly picked herbs in a bowl. Sprinkle with flowers. Flowers should be picked off their stems and sepals but not washed. It's important not to pick the ones next to a road or flowers that have been sprayed. Young scented geranium leaves and flowers make a good addition but only in very small amounts.

If you have access to thin asparagus shoots called "sparrow grass", add them after giving them a short blast in the microwave. They are delicious. Add the vinaigrette just before serving.

HELMSLEY WALLED GARDEN CAFÉ DRESSING

The Helmsley Walled Garden Café, set in the tranquillity of the Walled Garden, offers a simple but delicious vegetarian menu of fresh garden salads, soups and a wide selection of tasty cakes. A trio of salads is served with an organic bread roll and unusual patés, such as pear and stilton pâté, and red lentil, sundried tomato and Welsh mead pâté. Special dietary needs are catered for wherever possible. The Café's salad dressing is much in demand. Monica Gripaios who runs the Café has let us have the recipe.

1 tbsp wholegrain mustard
4 tbsp clear honey
1 tsp salt ground black pepper
50ml (2floz) balsamic vinegar
50ml (2floz) red wine vinegar
300ml (11floz) good virgin olive oil

Mix the ingredients well. Delicious when served with fresh salads.

DILL AND AVOCADO DRESSING

This is another excellent option for a salad dressing, from Margery Turner. It goes well with green salads, tomatoes, cold salmon, barbecued fish, prawns and rice or pasta salads.

1 avocado pear, stone removed and skinned
1 level tbsp honey
4 tbsp oil
2 tbsp lemon juice
3 tbsp fresh dill, chopped

Blend the avocado flesh with the rest of the ingredients until smooth. Use immediately.

ORIENTAL CRAB RICE SALAD

SERVES 1 OR 2

Martin Vander Weyer, the author and playwright, and the Director of the Helmsley Arts Centre, is a former Chairman of the Board of Trustees of the Walled Garden Trust. He does his own cooking and writes about this recipe: "One of the pleasures of life in Helmsley is the Friday market. My golden retriever, Gregory, and I follow an unvarying ritual of visiting first the cheesemonger, Tony, who gives Gregory a slice of cheddar, and then the fishmongers, Steve and Rachel. If there are crabs to be had, I buy one for lunch…This is my way of making one modest crab into a more substantial dish for one person or a good starter for two. It has oriental overtones, but it does not pretend to be authentic."

1 small-to-medium-sized dressed crab
½ cup basmati rice
2 spring onions, finely chopped
4-6 cherry vine tomatoes, quartered
1 small piece of fresh ginger, very finely chopped
lemon juice
sesame oil
salt and pepper
1 tbsp mayonnaise
sweet chilli sauce
handful of mixed salad leaves
coriander, chopped

Cook half a cup of good basmati rice and leave to cool but not to go cold. Take the crab apart and save all the white meat from the body, legs and claws, and as much of the brown meat as you like. Mix the crab meat and rice together with spring onions, cherry vine tomatoes and ginger. Add salt, pepper, lemon juice and a few scattered drops of sesame oil to taste: the idea is not to overpower the flavour of the crab itself, which should infuse the warm rice.

Mix together in a bowl a tablespoon of mayonnaise and some sweet chilli sauce to taste – more chilli if you like it hot. Serve the crab rice mixture on a bed of mixed salad leaves, garnished with chopped coriander, or the green part of the spring onions, and with the chilli mayonnaise on the side.

COUSCOUS SALAD

SERVES 4

The Walled Garden Café serves this salad as a lunch treat. There you can enjoy it in the peaceful atmosphere of the garden, surrounded by plants.

2 cups of couscous soaked in 2 cups of cold water for 20 minutes
½ cucumber, chopped finely
4 spring onions, chopped finely
fresh mint and parsley, chopped, to taste
4 tbsp sundried tomatoes
4 tbsp black olives, sliced
juice of ½ lemon
salt, pepper and olive oil to taste
125g (4oz) feta cheese, cubed (optional)

Mix the ingredients well. Feta cheese goes well with it.

WARM BLACK CABBAGE SALAD

SERVES 4

Black cabbage, also known as Black Tuscan Kale or cavalo nero, was only introduced to England in the sixties. It has a lovely nutty flavour and is among some of the less known vegetables, such as cardoons, Paul Radcliffe grows in the Walled Garden. All vegetables and fruit in the garden are seasonal and organically grown. They can be bought at the Garden shop.

4 heads of black cabbage
1 tbsp whole grain mustard
10-15 ml (1tbsp) lemon juice
40ml (2-3tbsp) olive oil
salt, pepper

Steam or boil the black cabbage *al dente,* toss in a vinaigrette made with whole grain mustard, lemon juice and olive oil. Season with salt and pepper. Serve at once.

WARM SALAD OF HAM HOCKS, BROAD BEANS,

WATERCRESS AND OLIVES

SERVES 5-6

Ian Carmichael, the well-known actor, who was born in Yorkshire, loves Duncombe Park. "I first arrived", he writes, "as a twenty-one-year-old subaltern in Duncombe Park in the middle of 1941, My regiment, the 22ⁿᵈ Dragoons, ...remained there in a brand new Nissenhutted camp for nineteen months, through one swelteringly hot summer and two bitter winters". Despite the awful weather, he retains the fondest memories of Helmsley and returns often. He takes an active interest in gardening and keeps a friendly eye on developments at Duncombe Park and in the Walled Garden. He has let us have his recipe for a substantial salad, which he himself describes as 'really jolly good'.

2 ham hocks
2-3 celery stalks
sprig of thyme, preferably lemon
   thyme
10 black peppercorns
half a medium onion, chopped
1 litre of dry cider

For the salad:
600g (1½lb) broad beans, shelled
   weight if fresh, but frozen are fine
two good handfuls of watercress
handful of small black olives

For the dressing:
2 shallots or half a dozen fat spring onions, finely chopped
1 tbsp each of (lemon) thyme leaves, chopped parsley and coriander
4 tbsp olive oil
2 tbsp wine vinegar
drop or two of honey to taste
black pepper
a little salt, depending on saltiness of ham

If the hocks are likely to be very salty – check with the butcher – cover with cold water in a large pan, bring to a boil, then drain and rinse. Otherwise just rinse them. Then put the hocks in a pan which holds them as snugly as possible, with cider, thyme, pepper, onion and celery. Cover with cold water and bring slowly to a boil. Simmer them over a very low heat – there should be only occasional bubbles glooping to the surface – for an hour and twenty minutes if you pre-cooked in plain water to remove salt, or an hour and a half otherwise. Remove from heat, cover and set aside to cool to room temperature. The meat should now fall away from the bone. Chop into bite-sized chunks.

Whisk dressing ingredients together, or shake in a screw top jar.

Boil or steam the beans, mix with ham and olives and toss the whole lot with the dressing and watercress. Arrange on a large dish or platter. Serve immediately with crusty bread.

SHRIMP, CUCUMBER AND POTATO SALAD

SERVES 4

A good summer lunch.

½ cucumber, peeled and thinly sliced
200-250g (7-9oz) new potatoes, boiled and sliced
250-300g (9-11oz) large shrimps, boiled and peeled
2 tbsp spring onions or chives, chopped
2-3 tbsp dill or fennel, chopped
3-4 tbsp yoghurt or sour cream
3 tbsp white wine vinegar
pepper and salt
pinch of sugar

Combine yoghurt or sour cream, vinegar, herbs and seasoning to a dressing. Fold in the shrimps, cucumbers and potatoes. Chill for one or two hours and serve.

Rievaulx

BROAD BEAN SALAD

SERVES 4

John and Lucy Warrack, teachers and writers who live in Rievaulx, have let us have this recipe. The salad is simplicity itself. It can be made with very young broad beans, or with older, tougher beans if you have the patience to peel each bean individually once they are cooked.

400-500g (1lb) broad beans, shelled
2 tbsp walnut oil
2 tsp lemon juice
salt and pepper
1 tsp sugar
dash of English mustard

Boil the beans in salted water until they are just tender. Drain them. Peel them if the skins are noticeable: this is labour-intensive but the best use of broad beans that got away. Dress them, if possible while they are still warm, with walnut oil – this is essential– mixed with lemon juice, salt, pepper, a very little sugar and a dash of English mustard. They will be good that day and just as good the next day if kept in a cool larder.

CHITRA SALAD

SERVES 4

Sir David Goodall, the Chairman of the Board of Trustees of the Walled Garden and a former Chairman of the Cheshire Foundation, has had a lifelong interest in watercolour painting. He is an accomplished amateur who, among other things, has illustrated his book 'Ryedale Pilgrimage'. As a diplomatic couple, he and his wife travelled the world. They were given this recipe by their Sri Lankan nanny, Chitra Arachchi. It is a favourite of the family and excellent as a side salad with curry or cold meats.

1 medium onion
2 carrots
2 or 3 tomatoes
½ cucumber
1 chillie
juice of 2 lemons
good helping of salt
black pepper, freshly ground
½ tsp dry mustard

Cut up all the vegetables thinly. Then add lemon juice, salt, pepper and mustard. Leave for half an hour before eating.

CHRISTMAS SALAD

SERVES 4

Cabbage is a vegetable of the ancient world. Red cabbage has been around at least since the sixteenth century. It is a traditional accompaniment for a Christmas goose. This salad has a number of typically festive ingredients and is particularly good when served with turkey or game.

200g (7oz) red cabbage, finely sliced
2-3 beetroot, boiled and cubed
1 apple, ideally cox, peeled and diced
1 celery stick, finely sliced
handful of raisins or dried
  cranberries
4-5 walnuts, shelled and chopped
  (optional)
1 sweet onion, diced

For the dressing:
2-3 tbsp olive oil
2-3 tbsp red wine vinegar
1 tsp ground cinnamon
2 tsp sugar
white pepper, salt

Combine the salad ingredients in a bowl. Make the dressing and pour it over. Let macerate in the refrigerator for at least six hours to soften the red cabbage.

Main courses are the *pièce de résistance* of every cook book. This collection owes a lot to the inventiveness of professional cooks in the area and the practical minds of home cooks. The recipes range from the simple and straightforward to the more intricate and sophisticated. They cater for all levels of culinary expertise and give an insight into gastronomic riches in the region There is a growing emphasis on food from local sources be it meat, venison, fish, vegetables or cheeses. It can be said that good food is being offered with pride in many places, making it a pleasure to go out for a meal.

BEEF AND VEAL

SUNDAY ROAST

Serves 10-12

Sunday roast is a mainstay of nearly all Yorkshire inns. Beef, pork or lamb are used; but the English are supposed to excel at roasting beef, so much so that the French still call them, in a partly affectionate, partly derogatory way, 'rosbifs'. Roast beef and Yorkshire pudding is a national icon. At the Durham Ox in Crayke, rib of beef is used as a cut, whereas, at home, the owner Teresa Ibbotson uses a flat sirloin. Two kilos (4 pounds) is the minimum size for the joint to ensure successful roasting. Teresa Ibbotson writes: "The basis of a good roast lies with your butcher…There are a few very good family butchers left in the area… The meat must have fat on the outside, marbling on the inside and be well hung. Buy twice as much as you need – a small joint is hardly worth the effort".

2 kilos (4lb) rib of beef or sirloin
beef dripping or oil – enough to cover the bottom of the pan
salt and pepper

Rub the beef with salt and pepper. Heat the fat in a roasting pan and brown the meat all over to seal, on the top of the stove. Transfer to a hot oven at 220°C/425°F/gas mark 7 and cook for 30 minutes per kilo/15 minutes per pound. Remove from the oven and leave to stand for at least an hour on a warm dish. This makes for rare beef.

DUNCOMBE PARK

BEEF STEW WITH PRUNES

SERVES 6

A wonderfully comforting stew – very rich and succulent – from the kitchen of Lady Feversham.

900g (2lb) lean stewing beef, cubed
4 tbsp olive oil
375g (13oz) shallots, peeled
3 cloves of garlic, crushed
5 rashers of streaky unsmoked bacon, chopped
425ml (¾pt) full-bodied red wine
2 beef stock cubes
3 tbsp plain flour
2 bay leaves
5 tbsp parsley, chopped
150g (7oz) button mushrooms
½ tin of anchovies and their oil (have faith!)
150g (7oz) prunes, stoned
3 strips of orange peel, about 7-8cm (3") long
2 tbsp thyme, chopped

Heat the oil in a casserole and brown the beef. Add shallots, bacon and garlic and fry for 4-5 minutes. Stir in the flour, then add wine, stock cubes, anchovies, bay leaves and orange peel. Season well. Bring nearly to the boil, cover and cook in a preheated oven at 180°C/350°F/gas mark 4 for one and a half hours. Add the prunes and mushrooms and cook for a further 30 minutes. Scatter with a handful of finely chopped parsley and thyme before serving. Particularly good when served with a potato and celeriac mash. Like most stews, this is much better the next day, allowing the flavours to mingle and meld.

NICHOLAS RHEA'S CHILLI CON CARNE

SERVES 4

Nicholas Rhea is the pseudonym of Peter N. Walker who lives near Helmsley and over the last thirty years has been writing books drawing on his experiences in the police force and his love for Yorkshire. He is the author of some 115 books, including the Constable series on which the popular TV drama 'Heartbeat', produced by Yorkshire Television, is based. He also writes crime novels and books about Yorkshire, in addition to contributing columns on rural topics to local newspapers. At home, he also makes a regular contribution by cooking some of the meals. He has let us have this practical and tasty recipe.

500g (1lb) minced beef
1 medium onion, chopped
2 tbsp oil
1 tsp sugar
1½ tsp chilli powder or to taste
salt to taste
1 tbsp flour
1x400g (14oz) can of tomatoes, either peeled or chopped
1x420g (15oz) can of red kidney beans

Place the onion in a deep casserole dish and fry gently on a low heat until the onion is soft. Add the minced beef and transfer to a high heat to brown the meat quickly, stirring the whole time. When it is brown, add the chilli powder, the sugar and the salt, stirring them well into the meat. Nicholas Rhea uses one and a half teaspoonful of chilli, but suit your taste and beware of the size of the teaspoons! Add these ingredients either while the dish is cooking or removed temporarily from the heat. Then sprinkle the flour on the mixture and cook for one more minute. You might care to leave the flour on the surface and not stir. Nicholas suggests you stir for a single minute to prevent the contents from sticking to the pan. Then add the tin of beans and the tin of tomatoes and their juices. Mix them well with the other ingredients and bring to the boil, stirring all the time. Once the chilli con carne is boiling, the dish can be covered and left to simmer for ten or fifteen minutes. Then place the covered dish in a preheated moderate oven and cook slowly for about an hour and a quarter – give or take about fifteen minutes -, stirring occasionally. Serve with boiled rice.

SPAGHETTI BOLOGNESE

SERVES 4

Piers Paul Read, the third son of Sir Herbert Read, the poet and art critic, was born on a farm at Muscoates Grange near Kirkbymoorside. He is a well-known author in his own right. His childhood in North Yorkshire in the 1950's inspired his novel 'The Upstart' and his school days at Gilling Castle and Ampleforth 'Monk Dawson'. He is also the author of 'Alive. The Story of the Andes Survivors'. His most recent novel was 'Alice in Exile' – again with a connection to Yorkshire. His authorised biography of Alec Guinness was published in October 2003. He has let us have this special recipe. "The only dish that my children consider I prepare better than my wife", he says, "is the sauce for spaghetti Bolognese. My wife says that no one from Bologna would make it the same way." There is something to her comment: Spaghetti Bolognese has become a much beloved standby of Anglo-Saxon cuisine after World War II, based on the Italian dish 'Ragù alla Bolognese' which is usually served in Italy with tagliatelle or green lasagna. His version is unusual in that it is cooked in the oven.

1-2 tbsp olive oil
1-2 onions, chopped
500g (1lb) lean minced beef
3-4 rashers of bacon, snipped
1 x 400g tin chopped tomatoes
1 cube chicken stock
1 clove of garlic, squeezed
salt and pepper
glass of red wine
sprinkling of mixed herbs
½ tube tomato paste
400g spaghetti

Chop up one or two onions; fry them in olive oil in a heavy casserole dish. At the same time, brown the lean mince, also in olive oil, in a frying pan. Cut snippets of bacon into the frying onions. When mince, onion and bacon are all brown, drain off surplus liquid from the mince and mix the mince into the casserole. Add a tin of chopped tomatoes, a cube of chicken stock, a squeezed clove of garlic, salt, pepper, a glass of red wine, a sprinkling of mixed herbs and half a tube of tomato paste. Stir everything together and bake in the oven on a low heat (100°C/200°F) for one and a half hours. Check its progress every half hour and add water if it gets too dry.

Cook the spaghetti in a lot of boiling water with a few drops of olive oil and serve with the sauce.

STUFFED BREAST OF VEAL

SERVES 6-8

The recipe has the heading "To Make a pudding in a Breast of Veal" in an eighteenth century cookbook believed to come from the kitchens of Duncombe Park where generations of cooks recorded by hand examples of what was then considered good cooking. The entries are often signed and sometimes dated. The book goes back to the early years of the eighteenth century, just after Charles Duncombe had built Duncombe Park to the designs of William Wakefield with some possible input by Sir John Vanbrugh who then worked on nearby Castle Howard. Just as quality materials and good workmanship were used in the construction of the house, so too in the kitchen: the cook book exudes an air of stability and good living. The recipes depict a life style where good food mattered. They sometimes call for the use of expensive ingredients but are never over the top. Quite a number of them can still be used today but quantities need to be adjusted since contemporary households are much smaller. Here is a modernised version of the recipe from the earlier part of the cook book which makes a very good Sunday lunch.

3000g(6½ lb) veal brisket, deboned and parboiled
250 ml (½ pt) white wine

For the stuffing:
50g (2oz) stale white bread diced
handful of 'sweet herbs' such as parsley, thyme or tarragon, chopped
1 medium onion chopped
1 tbsp lemon peel grated
150g (5oz) lean bacons diced

50g suet shredded
salt and pepper
¼ tsp ground allspice
½ tsp ground nutmeg
2 egg yolks
1 egg white
250 ml (½ pt) cream
250g (½ pt) flour

For the garnish:
1 lemon sliced
pickled gherkin slices

For this recipe you need to order from your butcher a good size brisket of veal. Ask him to remove all bones and cartilage so that a large pocket is formed in the meat. Parboil it and let cool.

To make the stuffing, combine, in a bowl, bread crumbs, herbs, onion, lemon peel, bacon and suet. Season with salt and pepper. Add allspice and nutmeg. In a larger bowl, beat the eggs together with the cream and then gradually work in the flour. Add the mixture of bread crumbs, bacon etc to this and work it through. Put this filling into the pocket and stitch it up with kitchen thread or close it with skewers. Place in a roasting tin with the white wine in a preheated oven at 200°C/400°F/gas mark 6 and bake for one and a half hours, basting it frequently. Garnish with lemon slices and gherkins. Serve sliced with a purée of potatoes and celeriac and with glazed carrots.

HERBED ESCALOPES OF VEAL WITH LAVENDER GRAVY

SERVES 8

TJ Drew of the Appletree in Marton recommends this dish for the tenderness and superbly subtle flavour of the veal and the aromatic flavours of the lavender gravy.

For the escalopes:
**1 kg veal (sirloin), thinly sliced across
   the grain**

½ medium loaf of white bread
handful fresh parsley, chopped
handful fresh coriander, chopped
**handful of fresh lemon balm,
   chopped**
handful of fresh tarragon, chopped
generous pinch of fresh thyme

2 cups seasoned flour
5 eggs, whisked

For the lavender gravy:
**handful of young lavender shoots,
   leaves removed and finely
   chopped or bruised**
**400ml (14floz) good home-made
   stock, using veal bones and a glass
   of white wine**

Remove any excess fat from the veal and slice it thinly against the grain. Blend white bread, parsley, coriander, lemon balm, tarragon and thyme together in a food processor to obtain fine green breadcrumbs. Dip the slices of veal into the seasoned flour and pat off extra flour. Then dip the floured veal into the eggs and finally into the breadcrumb mix. The crumbs should coat the veal well. To cook, simply shallow fry for just one minute on each side. Remove and drain on kitchen towel before serving.

Meanwhile, heat the stock and thicken slightly or reduce to desired consistency. Add the finely chopped lavender – the 'Papillon' variety is good to use – and simmer for 5-10 minutes until the right strength is reached and the taste of the gravy is to your liking. Remove all the lavender, because if left in the gravy, it will impart a bitter aftertaste. Add more finely chopped fresh lavender to the gravy before you serve it. For a really perfumed and slightly pungent flavour, infuse the lavender in vodka for several days to extract the perfume and add this to the gravy when simmering to burn off the alcohol.

CALVES LIVER WITH DEEP-FRIED SAGE LEAVES

SERVES 4

This recipe suggestion has been handed down from Glory Duncombe, the mother of the present Lord Feversham, who used to live in what was then known as 'Old Mrs. Duncombe's House', overlooking the Walled Garden. As an enthusiastic gardener she would have loved to have seen the Garden's metamorphosis.

For the garnish:
18-20 young, green sage leaves
1 litre groundnut oil

500g (1lb) calves liver, thinly sliced
125g (4oz) flour
2 tsp salt
2 tsp white pepper
1 onion, sliced into thin rings
1 apple, cored and cut into rings
1 tbsp olive oil
knob of butter

Heat the groundnut oil in a deep pan or a small deep-fryer until almost smoking. Sprinkle in the sage leaves and remove when crisp. Drain on kitchen towelling while preparing the liver.

Mix flour, salt and pepper and dredge the calves liver slices in the seasoned flour. Heat oil and butter in a different pan and fry onion and apple rings until golden brown. Reserve and use the remaining fat to fry the liver slices for 2 minutes on each side. Garnish with deep fried sage leaves and apple and onion rings. Serve with potato mash.

LAMB

The Star Inn
Harome

ROAST LOIN OF RYEDALE LAMB WITH A SALAD OF SAND HUTTON ASPARAGUS AND CREAMED GROSMONT GOAT'S CHEESE, LAVENDER VINAIGRETTE

SERVES 4

This recipe comes from the Star Inn in Harome, just outside Helmsley, housed in a cruck-framed longhouse believed to date from the fourteenth century. It has been an inn at least since the early nineteenth century. In the 1970s the Star won an Egon Ronay pub of the year award. Since 1996, the present owners Andrew and Jacquie Pern have boosted its reputation further while keeping its village friendliness. The restaurant earned a Michelin star in 2002 and has just been awarded a César from the Good Hotel Guide 2004.

4 x 110g (3½oz) lamb steaks from the saddle
2 x Grosmont goats cheese (or any fresh, soft variety)
12 trimmed, blanched green asparagus spears
200g (7oz) wild rocket leaves and soft garden herbs,
    such as oregano, chervil, flat parsley etc
1 dessert spoon grain mustard
pinch chopped lavender
handful garlic croutons –1cm dice approximately
50ml (2floz) grain mustard and honey vinaigrette

Trim the steaks, roll in the grain mustard, then the chopped lavender, wrap tightly in cling film and chill until ready for use.

    Cream the Grosmont goat's cheese in a blender for two to three minutes. Add a touch of cream if required to slacken, mix very slightly to enable piping, season with cracked peppercorns and a pinch of herbs.

    Next, to shallow-fry the lamb, which will have set slightly having been wrapped, undo the cling film and, in a little olive oil, cook the meat for two to three minutes on each side until a nice even crust forms. Lift out of the pan and rest.

Finish the plate by piping three pyramids of goat's cheese at triangular points three to four centimetres apart, arrange the wild rocket, garden herbs and croutons in the centre of the plate, the three asparagus spears between each pyramid on the outer side of the plate, then slice the lamb into about five to six slices and arrange it on top of the salad.

Dribble some extra vinaigrette around the plate and over the lamb to give it a little shine, garnish with a sprig of garden herb and serve immediately.

MARTON LAMB 'WELLINGTON'

SERVES 4

The Appletree Inn can be found in the peaceful setting of Marton, well worth a trip if you are after a good meal. The restaurant's most popular main course dish is their lamb 'Wellington'. TJ Drew has let us have his recipe. The secret in achieving a superb result lies in using quality local lamb.

4 lamb rump steaks, 150-175g (5-6oz) each, seasoned, any excess fat removed
1-2 tbsp olive oil
small block of puff pastry, rolled out into a square approx. 3-4mm (⅛") thick and cut into 4 smaller squares
1 egg, beaten
tapenade

For the tapenade:
2 shallots, chopped
3 or 4 handfuls stoned olives
2-3 cloves of garlic
1 tbsp parsley, chopped
olive oil

Quickly seal the lamb in a hot frying pan with a little oil, making sure all sides are well seared. Allow to cool while making the tapenade by blending shallots, olives, garlic and parsley together in a food processor. Add enough olive oil to form a paste. If it is too wet add a few breadcrumbs.

Smear a small amount of tapenade on each piece of lamb. Place the pastry squares over the lamb pieces and tuck the corners underneath. There should be no gaps, just one domed shape of pastry. Brush with egg wash and bake in a hot oven for 10-15 minutes if you like your meat pink, 20-25 minutes if you prefer it cooked through. Since all ovens are different, keep an eye on it. take the lamb, when cooked, out of the oven and leave to rest for 10 minutes before serving. The Appletree Inn serves their lamb 'Wellies' with rosemary and red currant jus as the flavours blend together well.

FRICASSÉ OF LAMB
SERVES 4

This is another historic recipe from Duncombe Park with the title "Friggacy of Lamb". Quantities adjusted to modern use.

750g (1½lb) leg of lamb
pepper and salt
50g (2oz) butter
1 tsp ground cloves
1 tsp ground mace
1-2 egg yolks, beaten
1 shallot chopped
1 onion, finely chopped
1 tbsp marjoram, finely chopped
1 tbsp parsley finely chopped
1 tbsp fresh breadcrumbs
50ml (2floz) white wine

Bone the leg of lamb and reserve the bone to make a stock. Cube the meat and season with salt and pepper. Put a little boiling water into a shallow pan and add the lamb pieces. They should not be covered. Turn them over to blanch on all sides. Drain the meat and add the water to the lamb stock. Sprinkle the meat with cloves and mace. Melt half of the butter in a frying pan and fry the lamb. Set aside.

Meanwhile make a gravy by adding the wine together with shallot, onion, marjoram and parsley to the stock. Bring to a boil. Thicken with breadcrumbs and cold butter cubes. Stir well and take off the heat. Gradually add the beaten egg yolks. Warm the lamb pieces in this sauce and serve, we suggest, with turnips and mashed potatoes.

PORK

KNUCKLE OF PORK WITH SMOKED BACON 'BOULANGÈRE' BLACK PUDDING BUNDLE, GIN-POACHED GOOSEBERRIES, JUNIPER CABBAGE

SERVES 2

Andrew Pern, born in Whitby in North Yorkshire, is an exponent of modern British cuisine whose art is deeply rooted in the North. He was formally trained at Scarborough College, then worked in and around the Esk Valley, close to his home. He adds a twist to traditional British style and anglicised classics, using seasonal produce from both local amateur and national professional suppliers. His use of all things local has, over the years, become his trademark, with outstanding success. The recipe below illustrates his skill in using traditional ingredients to create a very special dish.

For the hock:
One hock (450-500g/1lb total weight) cut into two portions (about 250g/½lb each), marinated over night in a mixture of seasoning, onion, garlic, apple juice, English mustard and sage leaves

Remove the two hock portions from the marinade, vacuum pack separately and steam cook at 89°C for 3½ hours.

For the bundle:
black pudding
sausage meat finely diced apple
finely diced onion
pinch of chopped sage leaves
pig's caul

Combine the first four ingredients and shape into balls 4cm across. Wrap in caul and bake for 5 minutes at 180°C.

For the gooseberries and sauce:
10 gooseberries soaked in gin for one week
½ litre (1pt) of Bramley apple juice and
200ml (7 floz) chicken glaze reduced by two thirds

Soak the gooseberries in gin for one week. Combine ½ litre Bramley apple juice with 200ml chicken glaze and reduce by two thirds. Then drop the gooseberries into this liquid and warm through.

continued

For the boulangère potatoes:
200g (7oz) finely sliced Désiré potatoes
50g (2oz) finely sliced onions
5g (1 tsp) finely chopped sage
20g (1oz) thin lardons of smoked bacon
250ml (½ pt) good chicken stock
50ml (2floz) Bramley apple juice
100g (4 oz) unsalted butter
pinch of ground white pepper
pinch of table salt

Layer potatoes, onion, sage and bacon alternately in a heat-proof dish or cake tin. Season as you go with salt and pepper. Pour over the stock and apple juice until the potatoes are just covered, dot some knobs of butter on top and cook in a hot oven for 30 to 40 minutes or until the potatoes are tender and the top is brown and crusty.

For the juniper cabbage:
2 generous handfuls of 'curly kale' or a small Savoy cabbage
20-30ml (1- 2 tbsp) double cream
25g (1oz) mature cheddar or Lancashire cheese grated
2 juniper berries, crushed

Steam or microwave the cabbage until *al dente*. Simply add a splash of cream and two crushed juniper berries with a sprinkle of mature cheddar or Lancashire cheese. Season and serve as an accompaniment.

Assembling the dish:
Reheat the pork to an internal temperature of 72°C (140°F) either in a steamer or in the sauce.
Bake the bundles.
Cut out a cylinder of boulangère potatoes with an 8cm pastry cutter.
Check seasoning of reduced sauce.
Place the potatoes at the top of the plate. Place the cooked bundle on top. Put the pork off centre. Spoon the sauce and the gooseberries around. Serve the creamed curly kale either on the plate or in a separate bowl.

Serve immediately, perhaps with a nip of home-made gooseberry gin as they do at the Star Inn.

HOVINGHAM

LEEK AND BACON PUDDING
SERVES 6-8

Neil Booth comes from Northumberland and has lived for nearly forty years in Hovingham while working first as an engineer in Middlesborough in the steel works and later making chocolates for Rowntrees in York. He admired Alison Ticehurst for her extraordinary vision and determination to revive the Walled Garden and became first a casual volunteer and eventually a Trustee. Among many other things, he has a passion for leek cultivation.

He has let us have his recipe for leek pudding which is, as he points out, "not for the faint hearts and demands a healthy appetite. Walk for five or six miles, split a pile of logs, dig a trench for next year's crop: the choice is yours". The dish has its origins in the coal mining areas of Durham and Northumberland where almost every allotment and cottage garden once contained a leek bed and where the tradition of leek growing is still strong. Neil also thinks suet puddings, once a common place and now a rarity, should make a come-back.

For the suet pastry:
200g (7oz) suet
400g (1lb) self-raising flour
4 level tsp baking powder
1 tsp salt
225ml (8floz) water

For the filling:
1 kilo (2lbs) leeks, washed and cut
into 2,5cm/1" long pieces
250g (½lb) streaky bacon or ham,
cubed
pepper to taste

For the cheese sauce:
300ml (½pt) milk
40g (1½oz) butter
60g (2oz) flour
½ tsp English mustard
100g (4oz) cheddar, grated
white pepper

continued

First make the suet pastry by mixing the dry ingredients and the suet together and making a well in the centre. Add the water bit by bit to the well and work it in with the other ingredients until you obtain a stiff dough, which leaves the sides of the bowl cleanly. Put it on a floured board and knead with floured hands until smooth. Roll it out, about 7.5mm/¼" thick. Try to maintain an even thickness with no holes. Line a pudding basin with this pastry reserving a quarter for the lid. Pack this pastry shell firmly with the leek pieces and the bacon or ham bits. Cover with the pastry lid, crimping it together at the edges with the lining pastry and cover with a layer of oiled grease-proof paper topped with another of kitchen foil, making a pleat to allow for some expansion and tying them firmly to the top of the basin. To make a loop of string as a handle to help you lower it into the boiling water of a large pot is a good idea. Boil or steam the pudding for quite a long time, two hours at least, after which the pastry should have turned golden on the outside.

Now comes the tricky part: turning the pudding out onto a dish without letting it slump into an unsightly mess. As disasters do occasionally happen, it is wise to use a dish with a raised edge. After you have carried the pudding triumphantly out of the kitchen, it will collapse, in any event, under the onslaught of the eaters. Despite its superlative flavour, leek pudding is quite dry and has a rather insipid appearance on the plate. So, brighten things by serving it with colourful vegetables like carrots, beetroot or red cabbage.

To complete the dish, make a white cheese sauce while the pudding is steaming away. Melt the butter in a saucepan. Stir the flour into the hot butter and gradually add the milk. Whisking all the time, bring the sauce to a boil. Stir in the grated cheese. Adjust seasoning by adding white pepper and salt, if you like, and serve.

FAST TENDERLOIN OF PORK WITH MUSHROOMS
SERVES 4

Anne Lang who has kindly contributed this easy and delicious recipe for cooks in a hurry, likes to call it "Pork Quickie". She lives in Broadway Foot, a seventeenth century thatched cruck cottage set in a beautiful valley near Hawnby. An ancient stone barn has been transformed into a light and purpose-built art teaching studio where Ann teaches watercolour painting to groups of students who come to enjoy the tranquillity and beauty of the place while discovering their creative talent or learning new skills.

From start to finish the recipe takes about 20 minutes for preparation and cooking. It can easily be adapted to accommodate larger numbers of people and a variety of tastes by omitting or adding some ingredients.

600g (1¼lb) i.e. 1 large or 2 small pork fillets
225g (8oz) mushrooms, preferably chestnut mushrooms,
    cleaned and sliced
1 medium or large onion, thinly sliced
2 dessertspoons Dijon mustard
2 dessertspoon grain mustard
1 x 400g (14oz) can chopped tomatoes
1 x 400ml (14floz) tub crème fraîche
cooking oil
salt and freshly ground black pepper

Cut the pork fillet into thin slices. Pour a little oil into a heavy-bottomed frying pan, sauté pan or wok and, on moderate heat, fry the pork slices for 3-4 minutes until well sealed. For larger quantities, seal the meat in batches. Remove from pan. Gently fry the onion for a minute or two until soft, then add the sliced mushrooms and cook for a further minute or two. Return the pork to the pan. Add all the other ingredients and stir well. Let the sauce bubble and reduce a little. Serve immediately with pasta, rice or potatoes; calabrese, green beans or a salad; and a crisp white wine.

SLOW ROAST BELLY OF PORK WITH FENNEL AND GARLIC

SERVES 10

Father Leo Chamberlain, former headmaster of Ampleforth College, is also an accomplished cook. He has contributed this hearty recipe, giving quantities enough to feed a crowd of twenty, which we have reduced by half. Father Leo retired from his present post in December 2003 and is to be Master of St Benet's Hall, Oxford, from September 2004.

1200-1500g (2-3lb) piece of belly of pork, scored and boned
2 cloves garlic, crushed
1½ tbsp fennel seeds
salt and pepper

Crush fennel and garlic into a rough paste with a pestle in a mortar. Scald the rind of the pork with boiling water and leave in a cool place to dry. Rub fennel and garlic into the slashes on the rind. Roast on a rack in a hot oven for 45 minutes, then lower the heat and cook for a further two hours.

Serve with a green salad

SPAGHETTI VESUVIUS

SERVES 4

This aptly named, fiery recipe also comes from Father Leo.

1 onion sliced
3-4 chillies, deseeded
5 cloves of garlic, crushed
8-10 rashers of streaky bacon, chopped
1 tbsp olive oil
1x 225g (8oz) tin of chopped tomatoes
handful of fresh oregano, chopped
salt and pepper
400g spaghetti

Take a sliced onion and a handful of chillies, together with five cloves of garlic. Fry gently with bits of streaky bacon in olive oil until the onion is softened. Mix in the tomatoes with much oregano. Cook slowly for 45 minutes. Serve with the spaghetti cooked in the usual way.

FOWL

PIQUANT CHICKEN BREASTS WYTHERSTONE HOUSE

SERVES 6

Wytherstone House, a spacious Edwardian mansion and the home of Lady Clarissa Collin, stands by Pockley parish church, which dates from the 1870s and was built by the architect Gilbert Scott. Besides having to run the estate inherited from her father and having to cope with official duties – she was High Sheriff of North Yorkshire and Cleveland and is a Justice of the Peace and Deputy-Lieutenant – she has found the time to create and develop a magnificent garden.

6 chicken breasts
4 tbsp Mazola oil
2 tbsp Dijon or Tarragon mustard
2 tbsp Worcester sauce
1 tsp dried mixed herbs of Provence
pinch cayenne pepper
juice of 1 lemon

Make a marinade by mixing all ingredients (apart from the chicken) in a mixer or by hand. Make a cut crosswise on each chicken breast, put them in a fire-proof shallow dish and pour the marinade over. Leave for 6 to 9 hours or overnight, turning the chicken breasts and brushing them with the marinade from to time.

Heat oven to 220/230°C (425-450°F). Put the dish on the second shelf from the top for 35 to 45 minutes. By this time the chicken should be crisp and brown outside and succulent inside. This recipe is equally good with half a *petit poussin* per person.

STRIPS OF CHICKEN WRAPPED IN PARMA HAM
SERVED WITH A MUSTARD SEED SAUCE

SERVES ONE

The Black Swan in Helmsley opened its doors as an inn in 1642. With its façade of Tudor, Elizabethan and Georgian features, it is a Helmsley landmark on the Market Place. The hotel ghost resides in the Tudor part of the building. The hotel has provided a recipe for a simple and practical dish which is served on a regular basis.

1 chicken breast, skinless
3 slices of Parma ham
knob of butter
salt and pepper
1 tsp mustard seed
dash of brandy
125g (4oz) whipping cream

Slice the chicken breast into three pieces and wrap the pieces in Parma ham. Season. Place the parcels in a pan with hot butter and seal all sides. Place in the oven at 170°C/325°F/gas mark 5 for 7 – 8 minutes.

For the sauce, put the mustard seed into a hot pan and flambé with brandy. Add the cream and season. Cook for 2 minutes.

Remove the chicken parcels from the oven and place on a serving plate. Cover with the sauce and serve.

GREEN CHICKEN AND EGGPLANT CURRY

SERVES TWO

Hovingham is a beautiful greystone village set in wooded parkland. It is dominated by Hovingham Hall, an eighteenth century building designed by Thomas Worsley, with the well-known façade of the Riding Hall in the front and a famous cricket ground at the back. Next to the driveway leading to the Hall lies the church of All Saints with its pre-Norman tower and some of the finest early artefacts in the country. Sir Marcus, a former Lord Lieutenant of North Yorkshire and President of the Yorkshire Dialect Society, and Lady Worsley have now left the running of the estate to the younger generation and moved to nearby Park House where Lady Worsley, who has had a life-long interest in gardening, has created a new garden. She has given us this recipe for a spicy Thai dish.

500ml (18floz) coconut milk
1 tsp green curry paste
100g (4oz) chicken thighs or breast, cut into bite-sized chunks
1 tsp whisky
80g (3oz) eggplant, peeled and cut into bite-sized chunks
1 kaffir lime leaf
2 slices of fresh ginger or galangal
1 tbsp coconut cream
1 tbsp fish sauce
1 tbsp sugar
1 tbsp chicken stock powder
3-4 pieces of a de-seeded red chilli or to taste
5 sweet basil leaves

Heat about 150ml/5-6floz or a third of the coconut milk and add the green curry paste. When the oil starts separating out, add chicken and whisky. When the chicken is cooked, add eggplant, kaffir leaf and ginger or galangal. Bring the curry to a boil again and add the remaining coconut milk. Now put in the fish sauce, chicken stock powder, red chilli and sweet basil and remove the pot from the heat. Pour the contents into a serving bowl and decorate with sweet basil and coconut cream. This tasty and rather liquid dish is served with an ample helping of boiled white rice which is the focus of every Thai meal. Quantities and proportions can be adjusted to suit the number of guests and their appetites.

STUFFED CHICKEN BREAST WRAPPED IN PANCETTA WITH SHIITAKE MUSHROOMS AND LEEKS

SERVES ONE

This is another recipe from the repertoire of Paul Sutton, the former Chef at the Kings Head Hotel in Kirkbymoorside and previously at the Hazelwood Castle Hotel in Tadcaster.

1 chicken breast
50g (2oz) pancetta or bacon, thinly sliced
50g (2oz) butter
50g (2oz) herbs such as basil, parsley, thyme, finely chopped
125g (4oz) Shiitake mushrooms, destalked
1 large leek, sliced and thoroughly washed
50ml (2floz) olive oil
125g (4oz) butter
125ml (4floz) cider
2 shallots, finely chopped
1 tbsp coarse grain mustard
250ml (8floz) chicken stock
125ml (4floz) double cream
salt and pepper

If the chicken breast still has the knuckle bone, remove it. To do this turn over the breast with the skin side on the board and with a heavy knife chop through the knuckle. For the stuffing, place 50g (2oz) of soft butter together with herbs and seasoning in a blender. Blend until smooth. Stuff the breast under the skin with the herb butter. Do not pull the skin back completely. Place the slices of pancetta or bacon on a board. Then place the chicken, skin side down, on top and wrap the pancetta around the chicken. Refrigerate.

Heat olive oil and 50g (2oz) butter in a pan. When it starts to become hot season chicken lightly and place in the pan. Cook until golden and then place in a moderate oven for about ten to twelve minutes. Half way through turn the chicken over.

In another pan, place 50g (2oz) butter, add the chopped shallots and the cider. Reduce. Add the mustard and stir. Then pour in the chicken stock and simmer. When reduced by half, add leeks and mushrooms and cook for about three minutes. Pour over the cream and reduce by half again. Check seasoning and leave to stand.

Take the chicken breast out of the oven, put on a board and leave to rest for two minutes. Then slice it into three or four slices cutting on an angle. Take a deep plate and place mushrooms and leeks in the middle, pour over the sauce, arrange the chicken and serve.

CHICKEN TAGLIATELLE WITH PRAWNS IN A
GARLIC AND CHIVE CREAM SAUCE

SERVES ONE

Gillian and Robert Thompson have recently taken over as owners at the White Swan in Ampleforth. Robert grew up in Ampleforth and is following in the footsteps of his grandparents who owned the pub more than forty years ago. He learned his skills in the kitchen of the Black Swan in Helmsley where he also met his wife Gillian. As head chef at the Ryedale Country Lodge, he helped to put the Lodge on the gastronomic map. He has let us have this popular recipe.

1 chicken breast
1 shallot, finely diced
1 clove of garlic, crushed
200ml (7floz) cream
2 dessertspoons white wine
40g (1½oz) prawns
175g (6oz) tagliatelle
1 tbsp fresh chives
1 tomato, de-seeded and diced
olive oil for frying
salt and pepper

Cut the chicken breast into strips. Heat the oil in a frying pan and seal the chicken pieces, put in the finely diced shallot and crushed garlic and fry for 5 minutes. Add the white wine and reduce; then add the cream, bring to a simmer and cook until the chicken is cooked and the sauce is reduced to the right consistency. Add the cooked tagliatelle, prawns, chopped fresh chives and diced tomato. Bring back to the boil, season and serve.

PAN-FRIED DUCK BREASTS WITH BRAISED ENDIVES
AND MARSALA

SERVES 4

This recipe comes from Shallowdale House, a small guesthouse in Ampleforth with a large reputation for good cooking.

30g (1oz) unsalted butter
4 endives (chicory)
juice of half a lemon
150ml (½pt) chicken stock
4 large duck breast fillets
1 glass marsala
1 tbsp chopped parsley

Preheat the oven to 170°C/325°F/gas mark 3. Cut the endive heads in half lengthways and sauté in the melted butter over a moderate heat until slightly browned. Place in a small ovenproof dish, just large enough to hold them in a single layer. Season lightly with salt and pepper. Deglaze the pan with the lemon juice and add a few tablespoons of chicken stock. Pour over the endives, cover tightly with foil and place in the preheated oven for about one hour.

Score the skin of the duck breasts with a sharp knife and rub with sea salt. Place in a large dry sauté pan over a moderate heat, skin-side down, and fry for about 15 minutes until the skin is brown and crisp, removing the melted fat as and when necessary. Turn over and cook for a further five minutes. Remove and place in the oven for five to ten minutes while you make the sauce.

Deglaze the pan in which you fried the duck breasts with the marsala and add the remaining chicken stock. Reduce by about half and season to taste.

To serve, sprinkle the endives with parsley and place two halves on each plate. Slice the duck breasts thinly and place on top. Pour the sauce around.

FISH AND SHELLFISH

GRILLED SWORDFISH ROLLED IN HERBS AND PARMESAN

SERVES 2

Swordfish is quite a meaty fish, in some ways similar to tuna but with a more delicate flavour. TJ Drew of the Appletree Country Inn recommends this dish as a light lunch for a warm summer's day, ideally taken outside with a glass of wine.

approx. 290g fresh swordfish loin, cut into large, thin slices
200g breadcrumbs
small bunch of rosemary, thyme, sage, marjoram and chives
large bunch of parsley
lemon juice
olive oil
salt and pepper
50g (2oz) grated parmesan

In a food blender, combine all the herbs, the breadcrumbs and a little salt and pepper. Blend until you reach a colourful green crumb mix. Then stir in by hand parmesan, lemon juice and olive oil to achieve a moist but still crumbly effect. Brush the fish slices with a little oil and sprinkle the herb mixture on both sides. Roll each swordfish slice carefully so not to damage the flesh and gently press on any remaining herb crumbs.

Cook under the grill for no more than 5 minutes on each side. Cut through the middle just to check the fish is cooked and serve. As a main course, it could be served with buttered new potatoes and tomato salsa or, as a starter, with an orange and balsamic salad.

WHOLE TROUT

Lady Clarissa Collin of Wytherstone House has a passion for gardening and loves every-thing to do with the countryside. This is another straightforward recipe from her kitchen.

1 whole trout per person
lemon juice
good knob of butter per trout
1 tsp freshly chopped parsley per trout
salt and freshly ground black pepper

Place the cleaned trout in a shallow oven-proof dish. Add lemon juice, parsley, butter and seasoning. Cover the dish and place in the oven at 190°C (375°F/gas mark 5) for 20 to 25 minutes. Serve hot, garnished with lemon butterflies and accompanied by minted new potatoes and green salad. Alternatively the trout can be cooked in an aluminium foil parcel.

PAN-SEARED WHITBY COD WITH A WARM SALAD OF SEA TROUT, ROASTED FENNEL AND RED ONION

SERVES 4

The Fox and Hounds Country Inn is an eighteenth century coaching inn in the ancient village of Sinnington, which is mentioned in the Domesday Book of 1087. The village church dates back to the twelfth century. Nearby is a medieval hall which was later used as a private chapel of the Latimers. Catherine Parr, the last wife of Henry the Eighth, was the second wife of John Latimer. For a long time, the building served as a barn but was recently restored. Another important historic feature of the village is the Sinnington Hunt dating back to the thirteenth century. The Fox and Hounds Inn has not only provided the venue for hunt balls over the years but continues to offer hospitality and imaginative meals to their guests. The Inn has let us have this recipe.

4 x 175g (6oz) chunks of cod

For the salad:
1 bulb of fennel, cut in half
2 small red onion, peeled and cut into 8 segments
125g (4oz) sea trout fillet, diced
3 cloves of garlic, thinly sliced
6 tbsp balsamic vinegar
2 tbsp runny honey
juice of 1 lime
fresh basil and bronze fennel from the garden, roughly chopped
olive oil
4 tbsp ground sea salt
black pepper

For the salad, put the fennel halves together with the onions in a roasting tray. Drizzle with olive oil, sea salt and black pepper. Roast until golden. Coat the sea trout with olive oil adding salt and pepper. Fry in a hot skillet.

For the dressing, put the balsamic vinegar together with the honey in a pan and reduce by half. Take off the heat. Add the thinly sliced garlic and 4 tablespoons of olive oil. Season well.

Slice the roasted fennel up and add diced sea trout, roasted onions and herbs. Pour the balsamic dressing over and keep warm.

Then heat a skillet on the stove top and sear the cod skin side down.. Turn the fish over and put in a preheated oven at 200°C/400°F/gas mark 6 for roughly 5 minutes, until firm to the touch. Take out, put on a plate and serve the warm salad over the top.

FISH CAKES WITH LEMON BUTTER SAUCE

SERVES 10

This traditional recipe comes from Paul Sutton, formerly of the Kings Head Hotel in Kirkbymoorside.

125g (4oz) fresh salmon
125g (4oz) white fish
50g (2oz) fresh parsley, chopped
500g (1lb) mashed potatoes (Paul Sutton recommends red potatoes)
2tsp horseradish sauce
juice of two lemons
2 eggs
100ml (3½floz) milk
125g (4oz) flour
250g (8oz) bread crumbs
175g (6oz) butter
200ml (7floz) cream
125g (4oz) spring onions, sliced
2 tomatoes, finely chopped
1 litre (2pts) water
1 bay leaf
200ml (7floz) white wine
salt and pepper

Poach the salmon and white fish in half of the white wine and water adding the juice of half a lemon and a bay leaf. Poach until just cooked, Drain and leave to cool discarding the bay leaf. Peel the potatoes, cut them into quarters and boil in salted water. When soft, drain and mash until smooth. Put the mashed potatoes in a bowl and add the flaked fish, chopped parsley, creamed horseradish, salt and pepper to taste and just a few drops of lemon juice. Bind together and leave to rest.

Line a tray with baking parchment. Shape the fish and potato mixture into golf ball size portions (there are three of these to a serving). Leave to stand in the refrigerator for five to ten minutes.

Whisk eggs and milk in a bowl. Add seasoning. Put bread crumbs and sifted flour into two other bowls. First coat the fish cakes in flour. Shake excess flour off and dip into the egg mix until completely covered. Let excess drip off and then roll in bread crumbs. Put onto a tray and refrigerate until needed.

Cook in a deep fat fryer for two to three minutes and then place them in a moderate oven for six to eight minutes. **OR** cook in a pan with equal quantities of oil and butter until golden and then put them into the oven for six to eight minutes.

For the sauce, heat up a saucepan and pour in the remaining lemon juice and white wine. Boil and reduce. Add 175g (6oz) cold diced butter and leave to simmer. Pour in the cream and seasoning and reduce. DO NOT LET THE SAUCE BOIL. Before serving add sliced spring onions and finely chopped tomatoes.

Put a bit of sauce on a plate and then add three fish cakes per serving.

MOUCLADE

Serves 6

This classical Charentais mussel dish is a favourite of Lady Feversham. It evokes for her fond childhood memories of her French grandmother with whom she used to spend her school holidays. "The night before the school holidays ended", she writes, "to soften the blow, we were allowed to choose our favourite dish for supper that evening. When mussels were in season, I invariably chose this mouclade – a similar dish to moules marinières but creamier and saffron-scented. With a piece of warm, torn French bread, it seemed like a heaven on a plate."

2-2½ kilos (5lb) mussels, scrubbed
275ml (½pt) dry white wine
3-4 saffron strands
50g (2oz) butter
275ml (½pt) cream
5 shallots, finely chopped
3 cloves of garlic, finely chopped
3 large egg yolks, beaten
¼ tsp grated nutmeg
¼ tsp cayenne pepper
5 tbsp parsley, finely chopped

Put the mussels in a large pan, pour over the wine and cover tightly. Cook over a high heat for 5-6 minutes until all the mussels have opened. Strain the liquor onto the saffron and allow to stand whilst melting the butter in another pan. (Meanwhile, keep the mussels warm.) Add shallots and garlic and sauté gently for 5 minutes. Then add the liquor and all but 3 tablespoons of the cream and boil hard for 3 minutes. Allow to cool a little. Whisk the remaining cream into the egg yolks and add to the sauce, simmering for 2-3 minutes. After adding nutmeg and seasoning, pour the sauce over the mussels. Before serving sprinkle with parsley and cayenne pepper.

GAME

GRAPE-STUFFED PHEASANT

SERVES 4

The Pheasant Hotel in Harome near Helmsley has provided, appropriately, a recipe for pheasant. The Hotel on the site of the former village blacksmith's, incorporating two cottages and the shop, is run by the Binks family. Patricia Binks inherited this recipe from her grandmother.

1 brace of young pheasants (oven ready)
50g (2oz) butter
salt and pepper
1 tbsp sugar
350g (¾ lb) green grapes, skinned and seeded
small glass of red wine
2 tbsp sherry
25g (1oz) arrowroot
grapes to garnish

Cover the breasts of the birds with the butter. Season the cavities with salt and pepper. Sprinkle sugar over the grapes and soak in the wine for ten minutes. If you use seedless grapes you only have to peel them. Stuff the birds with the soaked grapes. Place in a roasting tin and put into a pre-heated oven at 180°C/350°F/gas mark 4 and roast for one and a quarter hours. When the birds are cooked remove from the pan and keep hot.

Meanwhile, make some stock by simmering the pheasant giblets in half a litre/one pint of water. Mix the sherry with the arrowroot to make a smooth paste. Pour the strained stock into the roasting tin and bring to the boil on top of the stove, stirring up all the meat juices. Add arrowroot and stir until smoothly blended.

Serve the birds on a heated plate garnished with grapes. Spoon a little of the sauce on top and hand the remainder around in a sauce boat. Canned or steamed pear halves filled with cranberry sauce make a good accompaniment.

LIGHTNING VENISON

SERVES 4

Wild roe deer roam the parklands surrounding the house at Duncombe Park. From time to time there has to be a cull to keep numbers under control, so there is a plentiful supply of venison for the table. Lady Feversham has developed this recipe which can indeed be prepared with lightning speed.

500g (1lb) venison fillet, cut into 8 slices, about 1cm (½") thick
3 tbsp olive oil
25g (1oz) butter
salt and pepper
100ml (3½floz) marsala
handful of fresh tarragon, chopped

Heat olive oil and butter in a frying pan until nearly smoking. Fry the well seasoned venison until well browned on both sides. Reserve and deglaze the pan with a wine glass of marsala and sprinkle the meat with chopped fresh tarragon. Serve immediately

VENISON SUET PUDDINGS

SERVES 8

This pudding is a close relative of the traditional steak and kidney pudding, the most English of all savoury puddings. The recipe has been devised by TJ Drew of the Appletree Country Inn in Marton.

For the suet pastry:
250g (9oz) self-raising flour
120g (4oz) suet
pinch of salt
water

For the filling:
1kg (2lb) diced venison – haunch is
   best-, dusted lightly with a small
   handful of plain flour
1 large onion, finely chopped
6 cloves of garlic, finely chopped
4 rashers of bacon, finely chopped
6 dried juniper berries
small bunch of thyme
2 bay leaves
½ litre red wine
fresh beef stock
salt and pepper

For the suet pastry, mix flour, suet and salt together. Add water and mix until you achieve a slightly sticky dough mix. Rest in the fridge until ready.

For the filling, brown the venison in a large pan and add onions, garlic and bacon. Then add juniper, thyme, bay leaves and red wine. Stir occasionally and reduce the liquid by half before adding enough stock to just cover the mixture. Cover the pan and turn down the heat to let the mixture simmer. Allow to cook gently for a couple of hours until the meat is tender and ready to fall apart.

Roll out the pastry to a thickness of 1,25 cm (½") and line a pudding basin with the pastry. You can also use small metal or earthenware dishes to make individual puddings. Fill with the venison mixture, but leave a space of 1,25cm (½") at the top of the dish. Then place a layer of pastry on top and crimp the sides together. Cover with foil and bake the puddings for about 40 minutes. Alternatively, you could steam the puddings in the traditional way.

When cooked, simply turn out onto a plate and serve with freshly cooked vegetables, red onion marmalade and a juniper and gin sauce.

WOMBWELL'S WILD BOAR AND PORK SHABAM

SERVES 10

The Wombwell Arms in Wass dates back to the seventeenth century. Before that the Cistercian monks of nearby Byland Abbey had a granary on the site. The inn was owned initially by the Stapylton family and known as the 'Stapylton Arms'. In 1896, it was sold with the estate to the then Sir George Wombwell of Newburgh Priory, from whose family it takes its present name. Cameron's Brewery, who bought the inn in 1924, sold it in 1987. Since then it has been a free house, now owned by Andy and Sue Cole.
The following recipe was created especially by the Head Chef, Andrew Hudson, for a 'Pub Chef of the Year' competition and has proved extremely popular. In case you wonder what 'Shabam' means: it is an amalgamation of the initials of the first names of the owners and the Chef.

40x28g (1oz) pieces of pork fillet
420g (15oz) wild boar and pork mince, available from Wensleydale Wild Boar Ltd
3 oranges, peeled and sliced
100ml (4floz) brandy
750ml (1¼pt) whipping cream
5 sweet potatoes, peeled and diced
2 large Bramley apples, peeled and diced
parsley

Flatten pork pieces to escalopines, approximately 10 by 15 cm (4 by 6"), and spread the wild boar mince onto half of them. Place the remaining escalopines in top to make twenty sandwiches. Set aside to rest.

Just cover the peeled and diced sweet potatoes with water and put on to cook Lightly flour the pork sandwiches and shallow fry in olive oil until brown on both sides. Set aside and keep warm.

Pour any remaining oil from the pan. Set aside the 10 best slices of orange. Add the rest to the pan and heat. Flambé with the brandy. Add the cream. Simmer the pork sandwiches in this sauce for 6 minutes.

Meanwhile, add the apple pieces to the sweet potatoes. When they are cooked, drain and mash. Place a dessertspoonful of this mash on each plate and place 2 pork sandwiches against it. Spoon cream sauce over and decorate with 1 twisted orange slice and parley.

It takes 40 minutes to prepare the ingredients and 25 minutes to cook.

EGG AND VEGETARIAN DISHES

EGGS HOWARD
SERVES 4

Castle Howard has what is probably the largest walled garden in Yorkshire, double as big as the Helmsley Walled Garden. Like many of the other walled gardens in the area, it fell into disrepair between the wars. The late Lord Howard of Henderskelfe revived a large part of it by creating a rose garden as a memorial to his wife Cecilia who died in 1974 at the age of only 52. It contains one of the best collections of old roses in the country. The walled garden also houses the Plant Centre, Nursery and Head Gardener's home with the remainder still awaiting redevelopment.

This seemingly austere egg dish from Castle Howard is an option for vegetarians. It can be served with braised lettuce (recipe below) or a salad.

25g (1oz) butter
½ onion, minced
1 clove of garlic, crushed
50g (2oz) flour
200-250ml (7-9floz) milk
4 eggs, hard boiled and chopped not
too finely
3-4 tbsp parsley and other herbs such
as chives, dill, fennel, tarragon,
chopped
2-3 tbsp grated cheese
1 egg, beaten
100-125g (3½-4oz) flour
100-125g (3½-4oz) breadcrumbs
salt and pepper
oil for frying

For the braised lettuce:
1 whole head of lettuce, tied with a
string
1 onion, chopped
oil and butter
200ml (7floz) water or stock
1 tbsp flour
salt and pepper

Melt the butter in a pan and add minced onion and crushed garlic. Cook for a few minutes, then add the flour. Continue cooking while adding enough milk to make a thick binding sauce. Then add the chopped hard boiled eggs, chopped herbs, grated cheese and seasoning. Mix well, let cool somewhat and form into cutlet-shaped portions. Dredge through flour, dip in the beaten egg and coat with breadcrumbs. Cook in hot oil until golden brown on both sides. Serve with a piquant sauce and a fresh salad or with braised lettuce.

Wash the lettuce in one piece and tie with a string. Then boil it in salted water for no more than 5 minutes. Drain well. Fry the onion in oil and butter golden brown. Reserve the fried onion and use the remaining fat to make a roux by frying the flour in it and adding to it some of the boiling water from the lettuce or, better, stock. Put the onion into the sauce, adjust seasoning and pour over the lettuce, taking care to keep it warm without boiling it.

The Star Inn
Harome

RISOTTO OF FADMOOR ORGANIC BEETROOT WITH A DEEP-FRIED BLUE WENSLEYDALE BEIGNET, WILD GARLIC PESTO

SERVES 4

This vegetarian recipe is typical of Andrew Pern at the Star in Harome. It combines fresh local ingredients with inventiveness to make a lovely meal. Seasonal fruit and vegetables are a hallmark of his cuisine. The Perns are offering, at their Corner Shop, local meats and game, fresh and smoked fish and shell fish, village and organic eggs together with delicacies from their own kitchen, thus proving that, even in today's world of supermarkets, there is a place for a well-run village shop.

For the risotto:
425g (15oz) beetroot thoroughly washed
250ml (9floz) good full-bodied fruity red wine (Shiraz or alternatively a splash of cassis)
50g (2oz) blue Wensleydale cheese finely grated
50ml (2floz) whipping cream
50g (2oz) shredded baby spinach
315g (11½ oz) par-cooked Arborio risotto rice
seasoning

For the beignet:
100g (3½oz) blue Wensleydale cheese
5g (1tsp) finely diced shallots sweated off
pinch of finely chopped sage
1 egg, beaten
breadcrumbs

Blend the ingredients for the beignet together and form into balls of 3cm diameter. Then chill for 20 minutes, egg-wash and breadcrumb. Set aside ready for use.

Boil the beetroot in a deep pan using 200ml of the red wine and cover if required with water to 'top up' the pan so that the roots are submerged (about 15-20 minutes), until tender, then peel and purée.

Put the par-cooked risotto into a thick-bottomed pan, add the beetroot purée, a splash of cream, the cheese and a little red wine. Bind together and simmer for four to five minutes, season, add the chopped spinach and taste. The mixture now needs to be quite stiff so it holds itself in a pastry cutter which acts as a mould. Spoon the risotto into the cutter on a warmed plate.

Deep-fry the beignet for 20 seconds or until golden brown, immediately drain on kitchen towel and place on top of the risotto. Garnish with sage and drizzle the wild garlic pesto around the base of the risotto, remove the cutter and serve immediately.

ARTICHOKE, KUMQUAT AND LEEK STEW

SERVES 2

This light stew is an innovative vegetarian dish from the Appletree Inn in Marton.

6 artichoke hearts (tinned will do)
6 kumquats, cut in half
2 leeks, roughly chopped
2 or 3 shallots, finely chopped
2 cloves of garlic, finely chopped
pinch of fresh thyme or rosemary
1 tbsp Puy lentils
1 glass of white wine
½ or 1 litre (1 to 2 pts) vegetable stock

Gently cook the leeks together with shallots and garlic in a little butter. Add herbs and artichokes. Pour in the wine and reduce the liquid. Finally add the kumquats and lentils and just cover with vegetable stock. Simmer for half an hour. Season and serve with a nice home-baked loaf, such as the Pink Peppercorn Bread (see recipe on page 107) or good wholesome granary bread.

BARBECUE

BARBECUED KEBABS

Barbecues are a great summer tradition in the Walled Garden. They bring together staff, volunteers, friends and other guests. Pat Hughes, who has helped with a number of these events, offers the following suggestions. Food on skewers makes cooking for large numbers of people easy. As a general rule, 150g (5oz) meat per person should suffice. Bread, rice pilaffs and salads are traditional accompaniments.

3,5-4cm (1½") cubes of lean lamb steaks, marinated in plain yoghurt, garlic, chopped mint and a little olive oil

3,5-4cm (1½") cubes of lean pork, marinated in pineapple juice, ground ginger, shredded sage and olive oil

3,5-4cm (1½") cubes of chicken breast, marinated in lemon juice, garlic, finely chopped spring onions and olive oil

3,5-4cm (1½") pieces of pork and chive sausage without further additions

3,5-4cm (1½") pieces of banana, wrapped in good quality bacon

3,5-4cm (1½") pieces of vegetables such as peppers, onions, tomatoes, courgettes, sugar snap peas, aubergines, marinated in oil, garlic, chilli, chopped herbs and other flavourings

Mix the marinades ahead of time and let the meat or vegetable cubes marinate in the refrigerator for two to three hours. Soak wooden barbecue sticks in water for 15 minutes before use. Then thread cubes on the skewers and brush lightly with oil. Barbecue until done. For meat this will take around 30 minutes, for vegetable kebabs about 10 minutes. Make sure that any meat, especially chicken, is cooked through.

Desserts is what the English excel at. English cook books over the ages are proof of that, offering an enormous range of delicious ways to conclude a meal. Clearly also in the Helmsley region, a good dessert is considered an impressive way to put finishing touches to a good meal, be it by serving a scrumptious winter pudding or a crisp fruity summer dessert.

MARZIPLUMS

SERVES 6-8

Another recipe, both delicious and ridiculously easy, from Glory Duncombe, the mother of the present Lord Feversham, who, besides being a knowledgeable plantswoman, was a superb cook.

500g (1lb) plums, halved and stoned
225g (8oz) marzipan
1 egg, beaten
handful of flaked almonds
250ml (½ pt) cream or crème fraîche
butter to grease the baking dish

Place the plum halves cut-side down in a buttered baking dish. Roll out the marzipan thinly and drape over the plums. Brush with the beaten egg and sprinkle with a good handful of flaked almonds. Bake at 180°C (350°F) for twenty minutes and serve with cream or crème fraîche.

BAKED GINGER PARKIN WITH RHUBARB RIPPLE ICE CREAM, HOT-SPICED TREACLE

SERVES 8

This is another recipe by Andrew Pern from the Star Inn in Harome. It again combines traditional Yorkshire fare, parkin and rhubarb, in an innovative dish with a twist. Matthew Fort of the Guardian made it his 'Dish of the Year 2001', describing it as: "A brilliant addition to the roll of honour of British Puddings. Tarty, tasty, spicey, racy and plum duff delicious! Served at the Star with a shot of rhubarb schnapps."

For the parkin:
100g (3½oz) self-raising flour
pinch of salt
2 tsp ground ginger
½ tsp ground nutmeg
½ tsp mixed spice
75g (3oz) oatmeal
175g (6oz) golden syrup
50g (2oz) black treacle
100g (3½oz) soft brown sugar
1 egg, beaten
1 dessertspoon milk

You need a 20cm (8 inch) square cake tin. Preheat the oven to 140°C/275°F or gas mark 1.

Sieve together flour, salt, ginger, nutmeg and mixed spice. Mix in the oatmeal. Melt down the syrup, treacle, butter and sugar. Simmer but don't boil. Then stir in the dry mix and blend together. Add the beaten egg and milk to the mixture to create a soft, almost pouring consistency. Pour into the greased tin. Bake for one and a quarter hours until firm in the centre. When cooked allow to stand for a quarter of an hour before turning out. This can then be served. However if kept in an airtight container, it will, like a good wine, improve with age. For best flavour leave for three weeks.

For the ice-cream:
200ml (7floz) full fat milk
250ml (9floz) double cream
½ vanilla pod, split and scraped out
6 egg yolks
100g (3½oz) castor sugar
250g (9oz) chopped slightly stewed rhubarb
about 50g (2oz) sugar to sweeten

Use the first five ingredients to make a crème anglaise mix, then cool down and churn in an ice-cream machine.

Meanwhile, sieve the stewed rhubarb and reduce the juices. Make sure the liquid is cool before adding it to the ice-cream. When the ice cream is nearly frozen, add the rhubarb pulp to give the ripple effect. Then turn off the machine. This can obviously be made in advance and kept in the freezer, no more than 48 hours to keep its flavour.

For the hot spiced treacle:
200ml (7floz) golden syrup
10ml (½floz) cider
½ tsp ground mixed spice

Mix the ingredients together and warm through.

LEMON AND ALMOND CAKE

SERVES 8

Bridget Gillespie is a well-known botanical illustrator with a longstanding relationship with the Helmsley Walled Garden where she gives botanical illustration classes. Her work combines great precision with a quality reminiscent of Old Masters. In 2002, she won a gold medal of the Royal Horticultural Society for a series of 14 watercolour paintings of plums. Apart from being a busy artist, she is also looking after a young family and has let us have this recipe which is very popular with her husband and children. She is not quite sure whether to qualify this dish as a pudding or a cake. She serves it as a dessert and any leftovers, later, with tea.

300-350g (10-12oz) i.e. 4 whole unwaxed lemons
250g (8½oz) unsalted butter or margarine
250g (8½oz) castor sugar plus extra for dredging
4 eggs
250g (8½oz) ground almonds
2 tbsp golden syrup

Weigh out 300-350g/10-12 oz of whole lemons, putting an additional lemon aside. Place the measured quantity in a saucepan, cover with boiling water and simmer for 1 hour. The lemons will be soft by then. Lift them carefully out of the pan so as not to split them and push them through a sieve into a bowl. Weigh the resulting pulp and use 250g/8oz. If you have more, you can increase all the other ingredients to the same weight but then you will have to extend the cooking time too.

Melt the butter or margarine in a bowl over simmering water. Then stir in the castor sugar, lemon pulp, ground almonds and the eggs, beaten in gently one at

continued

a time. Pour the mixture into a lined 20cm/8" loose-bottomed baking tin and bake at180°C/350°F/gas mark 4 for 1¼ hours. The cake should still be slightly sticky in the middle.

When cooked, allow to cool slightly and remove from the tin. Melt the golden syrup and stir in the juice of half of the remaining lemon. Pierce the surface of the cake with a fine skewer and pour the lemon syrup evenly over it, When it has soaked in, dredge with castor sugar and serve warm. Bridget's family like it with a blackberry coulis, cream or ice cream, warm or cold.

You can make a chocolate version of this which is even easier, half the effort and twice as naughty. Substitute for the lemons 225g/8oz of good quality plain chocolate and melt it together with the butter or margarine.

CARAMELISED APPLE TART
WITH CINNAMON AND MAPLE ICE CREAM
SERVES 8

This delicious take-off of a kitchen classic comes from Shallowdale House in Ampleforth.

For the apple tart:
9"(22cm) deep sweet shortcrust
    pastry case, baked blind
250g (9oz) caster sugar
6 Granny Smith apples, peeled, cored
    and chopped
200ml double cream
2 eggs

For the ice cream:
2 cinnamon sticks
350ml (12floz) full cream milk
6 egg yolks
150ml (¼pt) high quality maple syrup
300ml (11floz) double cream

Place the sugar in a deep frying pan and melt slowly over a medium heat until you have a dark caramel: it should just start to bubble and smoke. Remove the pan from the heat, carefully add the apples and stir with a wooden spoon. When the apples are coated in the caramel, pour in the cream and reheat stirring for about five minutes until the caramel is dissolved. Sieve the contents of the pan over a bowl and allow to cool for twenty minutes.

Preheat the oven to 170°C/325°F/gas mark 3. Arrange the apples in the bottom of the pastry case. Whisk the eggs into the caramel liquid and strain this mixture through a sieve into the tart case. Bake for about 45 minutes until the centre has set. Cool slightly before serving with cream or cinnamon and maple syrup ice cream.

The ice cream has to be made beforehand. Place the cinnamon sticks in a pan with the milk and bring to the boil. Remove from the heat and leave to infuse for about 30 minutes. Whisk the egg yolks gently with the maple syrup in a bowl. Reheat the milk and then whisk into the egg yolk mixture. Pour into a clean pan and heat gently, stirring until the mixture coats the back of a spoon. Pour through a sieve into a clean bowl and cover the surface with cling film to prevent a skin from forming. When cool, stir in the double cream and churn in an ice cream maker.

STRAWBERRY AND TARRAGON SOFT MERINGUE ROULADE
WITH LEMON CURD

SERVES 4

TJ Drew of the Appletree Inn in Marton has devised this delicate dessert.

Punnet of strawberries

For the meringue:
4 egg whites
200g (7oz) castor sugar
handful of fresh tarragon, chopped

For the lemon curd
100g (3oz) castor sugar
100g (3oz) unsalted butter
zest and juice of two lemons
5 egg yolks

For the meringue, whisk the egg whites until stiff. Fold in sugar and tarragon reserving a few pinches of the herb for the strawberries. Spread the meringue mixture on a rectangular oven tray of suitable size, lined with baking parchment. Cook in a moderate oven for about 20 minutes. Take out and allow to cool, then place in a fridge. If your fridge is not large enough leave it somewhere cool.

For the lemon curd, melt the butter together with the sugar and the lemon juice and zest in bowl over simmering water. Add the 5 egg yolks and cook until thick - for about 15 minutes. Allow to cool.

While meringue and lemon curd are cooling, chop up a punnet of strawberries and mix with a couple of pinches of fresh tarragon.

To assemble the dish, turn out the meringue onto a clean tea towel – preferably in one motion so as not to damage the meringue. Then spread the lemon curd across the whole of the meringue and distribute the strawberries over it. Take the nearest corners of the tea towel and roll the meringue into a cylindrical shape, cover and chill in the fridge. Try not be heavy handed when slicing it since it is a bit brittle. Put a slice on a plate with fresh strawberry coulis and garden mint. Add any leftover strawberries as a garnish.

This recipe can be varied in many ways, by substituting basil for the tarragon or raspberries for the strawberries. The lemon curd can also be varied by adding cream or using fewer eggs for a lighter effect. Using oranges for the curd makes for a delicious combination with the strawberries.

TERRINE OF FOUR SUMMER FRUIT WITH LIME SYRUP
AND CRÈME CHANTILLY

SERVES 12

Sinnington lies in an unspoilt little backwater 400 yards off the A170. It has a beautiful village green with a maypole and with the river Seven running through it. There are strawberry and raspberry fields nearby. So the Fox and Hounds Country Inn has provided this berry recipe.

3 punnets of assorted summer berries, preferably from Sinnington
575ml (1pt) sugar syrup, made by adding 175g (6oz) sugar to 575ml (1pt) of
**   water and boiling it**
8 leaves of gelatine or enough powdered gelatine to set ½ litre (1 pint) of liquid
dash of Pernod
2 drops red food colouring, added to the sugar syrup

For the lime syrup:
zest and juice of 2 limes
275g (10oz) sugar
150ml (5floz) water

For the Chantilly cream:
275ml (½pt) double cream
vanilla essence
sugar to taste

Soak the gelatine in cold water and squeeze out the excess liquid. Stir into the still warm sugar syrup, to which you have added a few drops of red food colouring and a dash of Pernod, until completely dissolved. Do not whisk. The syrup should have a pale pink colour. Add a few more drops of food colouring if necessary. Let cool.

When the syrup is cold, pour a thin layer, 0,5 cm (¼") in depth, in the bottom of the terrine and put into the fridge to set. Then place a layer of berries on top of it. You can use a mixture of them or one kind of berry per layer. Just cover with syrup and put back in the fridge to set. Carry on, layer by layer, until the terrine is full. Each layer has to be fully set before you can start the next one. Leave in the terrine till needed. This dessert is best made the day before.

HOT CHOCOLATE FONDANT PUDDING

SERVES 6-8

A lovely rich pudding from the Kings Head, Kirkbymoorside.

50g (2oz) cocoa powder
125g (4½oz) butter, melted
2½ eggs
2½ egg yolks
75g (3oz) caster sugar
125g (4½oz) dark chocolate pieces
125g (4½oz) plain flour
125g (4½oz) additional chocolate pieces

Sift flour and cocoa powder together. Melt butter and chocolate together. Whisk the eggs and egg yolks with the caster sugar. Stir the chocolate and butter mixture into the egg mix and whisk. Fold in flour and cocoa powder.

Coat small moulds with melted butter and flour. Tap moulds to get rid of excess flour. Fill the moulds up to halfway with the pudding mix and then place broken pieces of chocolate in the centre and cover with the remaining mix. Leave a little space at the top of the moulds to let the batter rise. Place moulds in a water bath and cover with lightly greased tin foil. Cook in a preheated oven at 160-165°C (310°F) for about 30 to 40 minutes. Check that they are done by inserting a pointed knife. Take the moulds out and let cool a bit. Serve with hot chocolate sauce and vanilla ice cream.

GRAPE PUDDING

SERVES 8-10

This is one of the favourite desserts of Sir David Goodall, the Chairman of the Helmsley Walled Garden Trust, and his wife Morwenna, who brought it back from India. When he was High Commissioner in New Delhi, their Buddhist cook Puranje used to prepare it for their official dinners. Once the Vineries of the Walled Garden are restored, it will be possible to use locally grown grapes for this dish.

900g (2lbs) green grapes, sliced and depipped
3-4 tbsp light rum
4-5 tbsp soft brown sugar
150g (5oz) plain yoghurt
275ml (½pt) cream

Put yoghurt, rum and brown sugar into a bowl and stir until the sugar is dissolved. Whisk the cream until stiff and fold into the yoghurt mixture. Gently add the grapes and spoon into glasses. Chill well.

The Hare
Scawton

CHOCOLATE MOUSSE

SERVES 4

The Hare Inn in the small village of Scawton, just off the Cleveland Way in the vicinity of Rievaulx Abbey, serves this dessert. Head Chef Chris Thompson has let us have the recipe.

4 eggs, separated
150g (5oz) castor sugar
200g (7oz) dark chocolate
250ml (9floz) whipping cream

Separate the eggs and whisk the whites until they form hard peaks. Add the sugar bit by bit until you obtain a smooth meringue. Melt the chocolate in the microwave and cool slightly. Combine the egg yolks with the melted chocolate while still warm and then stir into the meringue. Whisk the cream to hard peaks and fold into the mixture. Pour into glasses to serve and chill.

FIGGY PUDDING

SERVES 4

This fig pudding is served at the Appletree Country Inn in Marton as an alternative to the traditional plum pudding at Christmas time. Figgy pudding features in the well-known carol "We wish you a merry Christmas" and is a traditional Yorkshire Christmas dish.

170g (6oz) dried figs, chopped
300ml (11floz) water
1 tsp bicarbonate of soda
50g (2oz) butter
170g (6oz) castor sugar
2 eggs
170g (6oz) self-raising flour
a few drops of vanilla extract
custard or cream
fresh figs or rum-soaked dried figs (optional)

Boil the figs in the water for 5 minutes and add the bicarbonate of soda. Take off the heat and leave to stand. Cream the butter and sugar until light and fluffy, add the eggs and then the soaked figs. Finally mix in the flour and vanilla. Pour the batter into a baking tin or small dariole moulds for individual puddings. Leave enough space for the mixture to rise – about a third. Bake at 180°C/350°F/gas mark 4 for just over half an hour until the sponge is cooked. Turn out onto a wire rack to cool.

This light crumbly pudding is best served warm with a flood of custard, as tradition requires, or cream. Add fresh figs or rum-soaked dried figs for that "extra oomph".

"Oh, bring us some figgy pudding

And bring it right now!"

BYLAND CHOCOLATE ROULADE

SERVES 6

Jane Constantine has contributed this rich and elegant dessert as a suitable conclusion for a festive meal.

**175g (6oz) good dark chocolate, such as Menier or Bournville,
    broken into small pieces**
3-4 tbsp cold water
5 eggs, separated
225g (8oz) castor sugar
225g (8oz) double or whipping cream

Preheat the oven to 180°C/350°F/gas mark 4 and line a 340x240mm (13"x9") swiss roll tin with bakewell paper.

Place the chocolate pieces with the water in a bowl and dissolve over gently simmering water. Separate the eggs. Beat the yolks, adding the sugar gradually until a thick and mousse-like consistency is reached. Jane always makes this in her blender. Then add the lukewarm chocolate. Beat the egg whites and fold into the mixture. Put the mixture on the baking tray and level out. Bake at 180°C/350°F/gas mark 4 for 20 to 30 minutes.Allow to cool. When cold, cover with a damp tea towel and leave in the fridge for 24 hours.

Whip the cream and spread on the surface. Roll up the roulade, peeling back the paper gently. Chocolate roulades freeze very well; so Jane usually makes a double quantity for the unexpected.

COCKPIT LEMON SPONGE CUSTARD

SERVES 8

Sarah Balme lives with her husband Maurice above Kirkbymoorside. Both are keen gardeners. She is a painter and renders the surrounding landscape of the North York Moors in soft, muted tints. Her still-lives of fruit glow from the inside with colour. This is a recipe of her mother-in-law's served at Sunday luncheons.

450g (16oz) granulated sugar
50g (2oz) butter
grated rind and juice of 4 lemons
8 eggs, separated
4 tbsp plain flour
275ml (½pt) milk

Soften the butter and mix with sugar, lemon rind and juice. Add flour and egg yolks, then, gradually, milk and egg whites whisked till peaked. Put in a greased soufflé dish and stand in a baking dish or cake tin with hot water coming half way up the soufflé dish. Cook in a slow to moderate oven for about two hours. Check from time to time so as not to overcook the custard. (It can become rather rubbery when overcooked.)

20.VIII.03

DUNCOMBE PARK

BOILED RICE PUDDING

SERVES 6

This recipe comes from an old Duncombe Park recipe book written in many hands by cooks who worked there. The quantities given here are not the original ones which would have fed about twenty people.

75g (2½ oz) pudding rice
about 1 litre (1½-2 pts) milk
30g (1oz) butter
2 tbsp sugar
jigger of brandy or rum
2 eggs, beaten
¼ tsp mace

To serve:
butter
sugar
candied orange peel
medium to sweet sherry

Take the rice, boil it in just over half of the milk till fully done. Then gradually stir in the rest of the ingredients. The original recipe suggests boiling this mixture for another two hours, but it is probably easier to put it in an oven-proof dish into a gentle oven at 140°C/275°F/gas mark 1 for two hours. Garnish with candied orange peel and serve it up with butter, sugar and sherry.

STICKY TOFFEE PUDDING

SERVES 12

The Durham Ox in Crayke offers a wide range of desserts to its customers but Sticky Toffee Pudding remains their favourite. Attempts to remove it from the Sunday menu have met with protests from guests. "Grown men wept, beautiful slim young women's eyes brimmed with tears." Here is the Inn's recipe.

For the sauce:
250g (½lb) butter
500g (1lb) soft brown sugar
575ml (1pt) double cream

For the cake:
225g (8oz) dates, stoned and
  chopped
1 tsp bicarbonate of soda
575ml (1pt) boiling water
125g (½lb) margarine
375g (½lb) castor sugar
2 eggs, beaten
500g (1lb) self-raising flour

Make the sauce in advance as Teresa Ibbotson, the owner of the Durham Ox, suggests, by slowly melting all ingredients in a heavy- bottomed pan, stirring all the time. Bring to the boil and cook until the mixture leaves the sides of the pan. Never leave this sauce during the cooking process, keep stirring. This sauce will stand, covered, in the fridge for 3 or 4 days.

To make the cake, put the dates into a bowl, cover with boiling water and stir in the bicarbonate of soda. Leave to infuse and cool. Grease a 30x20x5 cm/12"x 8"x 2" roasting tin.

Cream margarine and sugar. Add the beaten eggs alternately with the flour, stir in the date mixture. Pour into the prepared tin. Bake in a preheated oven at 160°C/310°F/ gas mark 2-3 for 35 to 40 minutes until a skewer comes out clean. Serve, cut into squares, with the sauce and a big blob of vanilla ice cream. This quantity makes 12 generous portions and deep-freezes well.

LADY CLARISSA'S RHUBARB FOOL

SERVES 6

900-1000g (2lbs) rhubarb
a small jar of preserved ginger
sugar to taste
250ml (½pt) lightly whipped cream

Stew rhubarb gently with sugar and only enough water to cover the bottom of the pan, then liquidise. Add chopped preserved ginger and cream. Put in a glass dish and decorate with pieces of preserved ginger.

GOOSEBERRY AND STRAWBERRY CRUMBLE

SERVES 6

This is another recipe from Lady Clarissa Collin of Wytherstone House for a happy marriage of gooseberries and strawberries in which the taste of strawberries predominates.

500g (1lb) gooseberries
75g (3oz) sugar
25g (1oz) butter
150-200g (¼ to ½lb) strawberries

For the crumble topping:
175g (6oz) self-raising flour
125g (4oz) butter
125g (4oz) demerara sugar

Butter pie dish thoroughly, then add gooseberries and sugar finishing with a layer of strawberries. Make crumble in the usual way by rubbing flour, butter and sugar together and cover mixture in the pie dish with it. Bake in a hot oven for thirty minutes or so.

AUNT DODY'S LEMON TART

SERVES 6

This old-fashioned recipe has been supplied by Pat Hughes.

175g (6oz) shortcrust pastry
125g (4oz) unsalted butter
125g (4oz) castor sugar
2 large free range eggs, beaten
rind and of 1 large lemon

Roll out pastry thinly to line a 20cm (8") tart tin or dish. Prick bottom and bake blind for 10 minutes in a moderate oven (180°C/350°F/gas mark4).

Beat butter and sugar together. Add beaten eggs, lemon juice and grated rind. Pour this mixture into partly baked shell and return to the oven for about 20 minutes, until slightly firm. Serve warm or cold.

THE BLACK SWAN'S LEMON TART

MAKES 1 TART – 8 PORTIONS

This is the Black Swan's version of this classic.

For the sweet pastry:
125g(4oz) sugar
300g (11oz) butter
2 eggs
500g (1lb 2oz) flour

For the filling:
4 eggs
juice and zest of 2 lemons
150ml (5 floz) cream

First make the pastry. Mix cream, butter and sugar together. Add the eggs, one at a time. Mix in the flour and stir well. Refrigerate and use when needed.

For the filling, mix eggs, cream and sugar together. Add the juice and zest.

To make the tart, grease a 22cm (9") flan ring well. Line it with the sweet pastry and bake it. Pour the filling into the pastry case as fast as possible. Bake in a preheated oven at 120°C/240°F/gas mark ½ for 30 to 40 minutes or until set.

Serve with whipped cream and berries.

Castle Howard

FROSTED RASPBERRIES

SERVES 4-5

This is a light and delicate sweet, a good way to recall the pleasures of summer in winter. The recipe comes from the kitchen of Castle Howard.

225g (8oz) frozen raspberries
150ml (¼ pt) double cream
200-250ml (7-9 floz) yoghurt
1 egg white
2-3 tbsp vanilla sugar or castor sugar

Allow the raspberries to almost thaw, but not quite (one to one and a half hours at room temperature). Beat the cream until thick, but not too stiff. Fold the yoghurt into the cream and then the egg white into the mixture. Add the sugar, tasting for sweetness. Divide the raspberries equally between four or five glass bowls. Pour the creamy mixture over them and refrigerate until ready to serve.

GINGER AND KIRSCH MERINGUE GLACÉ

SERVES 8

Another inventive recipe for a sweet conclusion from Shallowdale House.

6 large home made meringues
6 small home made meringues
500ml (18floz) double cream
zest of a lemon
2tbsp castor sugar
4tbsp kirsch
5 pieces of stem ginger, chopped

Oil a deep round cake tin of about 9" (22cm) diameter. Whisk the cream until it forms soft peaks. Break up the large meringues and add them to the cream together with lemon zest, castor sugar, ginger and kirsch. Gently stir together and then place into the tin. Put the small meringues on top, pressing in slightly. Freeze overnight. Serve with fresh summer fruits.

BANANA ICE CREAM

SERVES 6-8

Anne and Bryan Cobb have, after a busy life in the military and on the farm, retired to an old cottage on the banks of the Seven in Sinnington. Anne is an expert cook and has let us have this recipe for a practical and delicious dessert.

250ml (½pt) double cream
2-3 ripe bananas, mashed
brown sugar to taste
2 lumps of stem or crystallised ginger, finely chopped
handful of ginger biscuits, crumbled OR a few grape nuts
1-2 tbsp rum (optional)

Whip the cream and fold in the rest of the ingredients. Freeze for an hour or so. Then give the frozen mixture a final whisk and return to the freezer for another 3 hours or overnight.

Ampleforth Abbey

STUFFED PEACHES

SERVES 6

Ampleforth Abbey accommodates those who come for retreats or conferences in a guesthouse called the Grange. The following recipe is taken from a collection of recipes compiled by the staff of the Grange at the request of guests. Readers are reminded in the booklet that St Benedict in his Rule admonished monks to "bless God and not grumble" about the quality or even quantity of food set before them.

12 preserved peach halves
125g (4oz) sponge cake
1 tbsp apricot jam
almond essence
6 tbsp peach juice mixed with 2 tbsp apricot jam
flaked almonds

Mix together sponge cake, 1 tbsp of apricot jam and a few drops of almond essence until bound. Form into six walnut shapes. Place each shape between two peach halves and arrange all peaches in an ovenproof dish. Spoon over each of them the mixture of peach juice and apricot jam. Sprinkle with flaked almonds. Cook in a hot oven for about 30 minutes or until the almonds are brown. Serve hot with cream.

This chapter deals with those tiny tempting morsels which can be served, with coffee, as a break during a tiring working day or at the end of a meal. For the fainthearted and calorie-conscious, they can even replace a dessert.

FUDGE

A cup of coffee with a fine confection is a fitting conclusion to a good meal. TJ Drew of the Appletree Inn in Marton has this recipe for fudge

575ml (1pt) double cream
600g (1lb 5oz) sugar
125g (4oz) glucose
vanilla essence

Boil all ingredients together until the mixture acquires a red tinge, then whisk until cool. Finally scrape into a well greased tray. Allow to cool and to set before cutting it into small pieces.

Be careful not to touch the fudge when still hot. Using thoroughly clean equipment and a deep, thick-bottomed pan, to boil it in, is essential. Keep an eye on the fudge: it has a tendency to boil over. You should end up with a rich smooth, silky texture but, if the sugar has crystallised, don't worry: you will have something akin to the Scottish tablet and still very nice to eat.

While whisking the fudge, you can add many other ingredients, such as chocolate, alcohol, fruits or nuts for added flavour and texture. If so, be careful as some ingredients will set the fudge a lot quicker than others.

FLORENTINES

Another recipe of TJ Drew of the Appletree Inn in Marton for a quick and easy after-dinner treat that also makes a great home-made Christmas gift.

110g (4oz) castor sugar
110g (4oz) clear honey
125g (4½oz) unsalted butter
350 g (12oz) flaked almonds
100g (3½oz) candied cherries

Boil the sugar, honey and butter until the mixture starts to colour. Then throw in all the almonds and cherries together. Be careful as this mixture can easily overcook or even burn. Turn the mixture over and spread onto a grease-proof tray or a pre-baked pastry base, or – more traditional – put little dollops of the mix onto the baking tray. Bake in a moderate oven for about half an hour. Take out and allow to cool, then cut into desired shapes. Keep in an airtight container.

This is a basic recipe that can easily be adapted, for instance by adding an extra handful of pistachios for colour and nuttiness or raisins for extra fruitiness and texture, or by dipping the finished confection into chocolate.

The Hare
Scawton

COFFEE CHOCOLATES

The popular Hare Inn in the village of Scawton serves these delicious chocolates made by Head Chef Thompson with coffee. They are quite easy to make.

200ml (7floz) double cream
125g (½ block) unsalted butter
685g (1½ lb) chocolate, white or dark

Melt the butter into the cream and bring to a boil. Add the chocolate and stir till smooth. Pour into a tray lined with cling film and leave to set. Cut into small pieces.

COCONUT MACAROONS

Macaroons are a well loved classic. Small versions are nice with coffee. This is Alison Ticehurst's recipe.

75g (3oz) flour
500g (18oz) desiccated coconut
500g (18oz) sugar
6 egg whites, beaten

Mix flour, coconut and sugar. Bind with the egg whites and place in small heaps on a greased baking sheet lined with baking paper. Bake in a preheated oven at 170°C/325°F/gas mark 3 for 20 minutes. Leave the macaroons to cool completely on the paper. It can be practical to turn the baking paper with the biscuits over and to moisten the underside with a damp cloth. The paper will peel off easily after a few minutes.

CAKES, SCONES & BREAD

Home-baking is still widely practised in and around Helmsley. People take great pride in their creations and in exchanging recipes. The ability to bake a good cake is not only a test of the skill of a housewife but plays an important role in day-to-day-hospitality. What could be better than having tea in the garden with a slice of cake or a scone?

SPICED LEMON CAKE

Alison Ticehurst was not just a committed gardener who started the revival of the Helmsley Walled Garden, she was also a champion home baker. She was aware of the intimate relationship between the English garden and teas. And she left a small collection of cake recipes. From her notes, it looks as if she had started a recipe collection for the Garden. This is one of hers.

100g (4oz) plain flour
1 tsp baking powder
½ tsp cinnamon
½ tsp nutmeg
100g (4oz) rolled oats
50g (2oz) chopped walnuts
2 large eggs
2 tbsp lemon juice
grated rind of a lemon
225g (8oz) brown sugar
150g (6oz) butter
½ tsp vanilla essence
3 tbsp milk

Grease a large cake tin and preheat the oven to 190°c (375°F). Sift flour, baking powder and spices together. Add walnuts and oats. Cream butter and sugar together till light. Beat in the eggs together with vanilla and lemon. Then fold in the flour mixture adding enough milk to make a soft dough. Pour into the cake tin and bake for about 30 minutes until risen and golden.

LAVENDER CAKE

The Walled Garden Café opened in 1996. Just before the opening, Alison Ticehurst asked Dawn Carvey to develop a range of both traditional and old-fashioned cakes for the Café. With the help of her mother, Jean Gill, she researched - and baked. They took a number of their cakes to the Walled Garden for all the people working there to try. This was the beginning of a longstanding relationship between Dawn and the Garden. She still bakes cakes for the Café.

This lavender cake is a Victorian cake. The Victorians were fond of the use of edible flower essences.

75g (3oz) soft butter
150g (5oz) margarine
225g (8oz) castor sugar
3 drops edible lavender oil
5 medium eggs, beaten
225g (8oz) plain flour, sifted
¼ tsp baking powder (optional)

For the icing:
100g (4oz) icing sugar, sifted
boiling water
crystallised violet petals

Sift flour and baking powder together and set aside. Line two 454g (1lb) baking tins or a 20cm (8") round cake tin with baking paper.

Cream together the fats and the sugar until white and fluffy. Gradually add the beaten eggs and finally fold in the flour. This recipe should not need a raising agent as the air in the mixture should make it rise but, to be on the safe side, you might want to add ¼ teaspoon baking powder.

Place in a cool place or in a fridge for an hour before baking in a moderate oven (180-190°C/350-375°F/gas mark 5) for 25 – 35 minutes, until a skewer comes out clean.

Allow to cool slightly in the tin before turning out. Keeps for 7 –10 days. Suitable for deep-freezing.

To decorate, make some hot water icing by mixing the icing sugar with a little boiling water. Spread the icing over the top and let it drizzle down the sides. Top with a few crystallised violet petals.

This cake depends on the use of **edible** lavender oil. If this is not available, you can use sweet geranium leaves scattered at the bottom of the cake tin. They give a very delicate flavour and can be peeled off the finished cake.

20.VIII.03   DUNCOMBE PARK

SAFFRON AND CARAWAY SEED CAKE

The Duncombe Park Cook Book contains a number of recipes for saffron cake. Saffron used to be produced in England then and was always an expensive spice since the stigmas of the saffron crocus have to be gathered by hand. People loved the spice for its subtle honey flavour and the beautiful golden colour it gives to dishes made with it. This recipe is a classical pound cake, providing for equal amounts of butter, sugar and flour, and predates the introduction of baking powder and self-raising flour. If you use self-raising flour you can reduce the number of eggs to five or six.

1 good pinch of saffron threads
1 glass of sweet or medium sherry or brandy
500g (1lb) butter
500g (1lb) castor sugar
500g (1lb) flour
9 (8) eggs, separated
15g (½ oz) caraway seeds

Soak the saffron threads in the sherry or brandy overnight. Cream the butter and then gradually beat in the sugar. Bit by bit add the sifted flour and the well beaten egg yolks. Then the caraway seeds and the sherry or brandy with the saffron. Fold in the stiffly beaten egg whites and pour the batter into a large buttered and crumbed baking tin. Bake in a preheated oven at 200°C /400°F/gas mark 6 for about an hour or until done.

YORKSHIRE PARKIN

The Yorkshire parkin is an ancient cake, most likely dating back to Celtic times. It has a close association with Bonfire Night. Originally probably made with honey and eaten at Celtic and, later, Christian festivals around the beginning of November. Guy Fawkes gave contemporary legitimacy for bonfires and thus the eating of the sacred Celtic bread shifted, together with the bonfires, from the Celtic Feast of the Dead on 1 November to 5 November. Dawn Carvey of Traditional & Scrumptious has let us have a recipe containing the essential ingredients for it: oatmeal, treacle and ginger.

2½ dessertspoons golden syrup
2½ dessertspoons molasses or black treacle
100g (4oz) margarine
100g (4oz) sugar
200g (8oz) wholemeal flour
90g (3½oz) oatmeal
1 tsp ground ginger
1 tsp bicarbonate of soda
2 medium eggs, beaten
milk

Line a 12,5cm x 22,5cm (5"x 9") tray bake tin with baking paper allowing the paper to extend above the sides of the tin. Set the oven at 170-180°C/325-350°F/gas mark 3-4.

Melt together in a pan the syrup, treacle, margarine and sugar. Do not boil.

Sift the dry ingredients – wholemeal flour, oatmeal, ground ginger and bicarbonate of soda – together. Add the melted mixture and then beat in the eggs, one at a time. Add milk to obtain a sloppy consistency. Pour into the tin and put it immediately into the oven for about 60 minutes, until a skewer comes out clean. Avoid opening the door for the first 45 minutes. Allow to cool before turning out of the tin.

Best kept for at least a week before eating. Serve buttered.

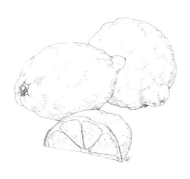

YORKSHIRE CURD TART

This recipe has been sent in by Hunters of Helmsley, a family-run delicatessen, which occupies a corner house on Helmsley Market Place and provides upmarket provisions for its discerning customers. A quaint façade richly decorated with flowers fronts an emporium of gourmet foods and fine wines.

225g (8oz) curd cheese
50g (2oz) margarine
50g (2oz) sugar
2 eggs
40g (1½oz) ground almonds
75g (3oz) currants
½ heaped tsp nutmeg
1 tbsp cinnamon
enough short crust pastry for a 25cm (10") flan ring
milk (if necessary)

Line the flan ring with pastry and chill. Cream the margarine with the sugar until pale and fluffy. Gradually add the eggs. Mix in ground almonds and eggs. If necessary adjust consistency with milk. Add nutmeg to the mixture. Pour the cheese mixture into the flan case and dust with cinnamon. Bake in a preheated oven at 200°C (400°F) or 190°C convection for about 40 minutes until golden.

ORANGE CHOCOLATE CAKE

Alison Ticehurst's collection of cake recipes was mainly destined for the enjoyment of visitors to the Walled Garden Café. She also baked a lot of cakes for sale, alongside with plants and other garden produce, on a stall at Helmsley Market to raise funds for the garden. She developed remarkable commercial skills in her efforts to make the Garden economically viable although, in the first years, it often teetered on the brink of failure.

175g (6oz) butter
175g (6oz) sugar
175g (6oz) flour
6 eggs
175g (6oz) chocolate powder
vanilla essence
2 tsp baking powder
juice of 1 orange

Beat the eggs while keeping back one egg white. Then, in a separate bowl, cream butter and sugar together. Add flour and beaten eggs alternately. Add chocolate powder and orange juice. Lastly, fold the stiffly beaten egg white into the mixture. Pour into a cake tin and bake in a preheated oven at 190°C (375°F) for about 50 minutes.

MINCEMEAT, APPLE AND WALNUT CAKE

Dawn Carvey who founded her business, Traditional & Scrumptious, in 1995 has, as a baker's daughter, baking in her genes. With this recipe she won a prize in a competition in the BBC Good Food Magazine. *It appeared in the April 2003 issue. "Pure", who sponsored the competition, are happy to see Dawn's recipe reproduced here.*

100g (4oz) "Pure" sunflower spread
100g (4oz) soft brown sugar
2 large eggs
200g (7oz) plain flour
½ tsp baking powder (see note)

1 small tasty eating apple, peeled, cored and grated
squeeze of lemon juice
200g (7oz) bought mincemeat
50g (2oz) walnuts, chopped
15g (½oz) walnuts, chopped for the topping

For the walnut crème filling (optional):
50g (2oz) "Pure" sunflower spread
25g (1oz) walnuts, finely chopped
100g (4oz) icing sugar, sifted
1 tsp pure vanilla extract

Mix the grated apple with lemon juice to prevent it from going brown. Add mincemeat and chopped walnuts. Stir well.

Sift flour and baking powder together and set aside. Note that Dawn uses her own mix of baking powder consisting of two thirds of cream of Tartar to one third of bicarbonate of soda. She considers this more effective than the bought varieties. It can also be used for gluten-free cakes

Line two 454g (1lb) loaf tins or a 20cm (8") round cake tin with baking paper.

Cream the sunflower spread with the soft brown sugar. Add the beaten eggs gradually along with the flour. It will probably look dry at this point but don't worry. Now add the apple, mincemeat and walnut mixture. Place the mixture in the baking tins and sprinkle with the remaining walnuts. Put in a cool place or a fridge for an hour.

Bake in a moderate oven at 170-180°C/325-350°F/gas mark 4 for 45 to 60 minutes, until a skewer comes out clean. Allow to cool in the tin before turning out. Split the cake across and fill it with the walnut crème filling. Suitable for deep-freezing.

For the filling, beat the remaining 50g (2oz) sunflower spread with chopped walnuts, icing sugar and vanilla extract.

ALMOND RICE CAKE

The recipe for this masterly cake comes from Pat Speed, a committee member of the Helmsley Garden Club.

225g (8oz) butter
175g (6oz) sugar
3 medium eggs, beaten
225g (8oz) ground rice
50g (2oz) ground almonds
a few drops of real almond essence extract to taste
a few almonds, whole or halved (optional)

Cream butter and sugar. Add the beaten eggs bit by bit and beat well. Add ground rice and ground almonds as well as the drops of almond essence. Mix all these ingredients for a few minutes. Have a 22cm (8") round baking tin ready, well lined on sides and bottom with grease-proof paper. Spoon the mixture carefully into the tin and decorate the levelled top with almonds, if you wish. Bake in a preheated oven at 190°C/375°F/gas mark 5 (convection: 160 or 170°C). Do not open the oven door until one hour has passed. Then, test the cake with a skewer. It may need 10 to 15 minutes longer.

GRANNY'S APPLE AND DATE CAKE

Another old-fashioned cake from Dawn Carvey developed under the auspices of Alison Ticehurst for the Helmsley Walled Garden Café. The Café is Dawn's main summer customer but she also supplies large quantities of Christmas cakes and traditional festive cakes to Lewis & Coopers, Northallerton and other shops and Christmas fairs.

125g (4oz) cooking apples, chopped
150g (5oz) golden syrup
2 tsp mixed spice
70g (2½oz) dates, chopped
75g (3oz) soft butter
75g (3oz) soft brown sugar
1 large egg
60ml (2½floz) milk
225g (8oz) plain flour
½ tsp bicarbonate of soda
icing sugar

Place apples, golden syrup, mixed spice and dates in a pan and stew over a moderate heat until tender. Allow to cool.

Sift flour and bicarbonate of soda together and set aside. Line two 454g (1lb) loaf tins or a 20cm (8") round cake tin with baking paper. Cream sugar and butter until light and fluffy. Gradually add the egg, milk and flour. Don't worry if this looks rather dry when all the flour is added. Add the apple and date mixture. The mixture should now look quite wet. Place the mixture in the cake tins and put in a cool place or a fridge for an hour.

Bake in a moderate oven at 170-180°C/325-350°F/ gas mark 4 for 45 or 60 minutes, until a skewer comes out clean. Allow to cool in the tin before turning out. Keeps 7- 10 days in the fridge. Suitable for deep-freezing. To serve dust with icing sugar.

GINGER COCONUT CAKE

Another recipe from Alison Ticehurst for a slightly unusual ginger cake..

125g (4oz) butter
125g (4oz) margarine
500g (1lb) plain flour
350g (12oz) ground coconut
225g (8oz) castor sugar
1 tbsp ground ginger
50g (2oz) candied ginger, chopped

500g (1lb) treacle
1 tsp baking soda
150ml (1gill) milk

Rub fat into flour and other dry ingredients and mix. Make a well in the centre to place treacle and soda, which you have combined beforehand. Gradually add enough milk to make a soft batter. Bake in a moderate (190°C/375°F) oven. Do not open the stove for 35 minutes. Test with a skewer before taking the cake out

TWELTH NIGHT CAKE

This is another traditional cake recipe from Dawn Carvey. Twelfth Night cake is made for the last of the twelve days of Christmas. Epiphany is associated with the three kings visiting the infant Jesus, but this cake and the festivities surrounding it still retain some elements of the wild festivities of the Roman Saturnalia where dice were thrown to choose a king who would rule against all conventions for a night. Twelfth Night cake traditionally contains a bean or other token. The person who finds the bean in a piece of cake is the bean king. This custom flourished in England for centuries.

Soak overnight:
700g (1½lb) currants, scalded in colander and drained
100g (4oz) mixed peel
50 g (2oz) blanched almonds, chopped
5 tbsp brandy

Cream together:
225g (8oz) butter, softened
225g (8oz) castor sugar

Add:
4 eggs

Sift together:
225g (8oz) plain flour
100g (2oz) ground almonds (optional)
1 level tsp baking powder

Stir the dry ingredients into the egg, butter and sugar mixture. Fold in the currants, peel and almonds soaked in brandy. Pour the batter into a 20cm (8") round cake tin and place in the fridge overnight. Bake in a cool oven at 170-180°C/325-350°F/ gas mark 3-4 for about 1½ hours, until a skewer comes out clean.
This cake would normally be covered in marzipan and decorated with a garland of glazed fruits and nuts.

LEMON CHEESECAKE

George Smith, the internationally renowned flower arrangement artist and horticulturalist, and his friend Brian Withill live at the Manor House in Heslington, York, famous for its distinctive collection of roses, iris, poppies and a wide variety of foliage plants including hostas, ferns and decorative grasses. Visits to the garden with its magnificent combinations of colour and texture can be arranged. Examples of George Smith's flower arrangements are on display in the house. George and Brian keep an excellent table and have let us have this recipe in support of the Walled Garden.

175g (6oz) digestive biscuits
85g (3oz) butter, melted

For the filling:
350g (12oz) cream or cottage cheese
125ml (¼pt) milk
500ml (1pt) lemon jelly
2 eggs, separated
4 tbsp lemon juice
1 tbsp castor sugar
125ml (¼pt) double cream, whipped
3 tbsp water

For the garnish:
2 kiwi fruit, peeled and sliced
handful of seedless green grapes,
** halved**

For the crust, crush the digestive biscuits and mix with the melted butter. Line a 23cm (9") cake tin with the mixture and press into place with the back of a spoon. Chill to set.

For the filling, dissolve the jelly crystals in water and 4 tablespoons of lemon juice over a low heat. Do not boil! Beat egg yolks and milk together and pour in the jelly while stirring. Return this mixture to the heat for a few minutes but do not boil. Cool until about to set.

In a blender, combine cheese and jelly mixture. Place the blended mixture in a bowl. Whisk the egg whites to stiff peaks, add sugar and whisk again. Fold in the jelly mix. Then fold in half of the whipped cream and spoon the filling into the crust. Chill.

When set, decorate the top of the cheesecake with kiwi fruit and seedless green grapes. Serve with remaining whipped cream

HUNGARIAN APPLE PIE

Under the name Almaspite this is a traditional Hungarian dish. George Smith, who is the author of the world-wide acclaimed book 'George Smith's Flower Decoration', and his friend, Brian Withill, brought back this recipe for an apple pie of a different kind.

500g (1lb) cooking apples
sugar to taste

For the pastry:
175g (6oz) flour
125g (4oz) white Flora margarine
1 egg yolk
2 tbsp milk

For the filling:
80g (3oz) ground almonds
50g (2oz) castor sugar
strawberry jam
1 egg white

For the garnish:
whipped cream
glacé cherries

Cook the apples with a little water on a low light. Combine flour, margarine, egg yolk and milk to a pastry. Use half of the dough and place it, shaped, into a greased tin. Cover with grease-proof paper and bake blind at 220°C/425°F/ gas mark 7 for 10 minutes.

For the filling, mix almonds and castor sugar together in a small basin. Take the pastry case from the oven and cover its bottom with strawberry jam and half of the almond and sugar mix. Then whisk the egg white and fold it into the apple purée. Reserve a teaspoon of the egg white. Place this apple mixture in the pastry case and put the remaining half of the almond and sugar mixture on top of it.

Then shape a pastry lid of the remaining dough and place it on top of the pie. Brush with the reserved egg white and sprinkle with castor sugar. Cook in a preheated oven at 190°C/375°F/gas mark 5 for 20-30 minutes or until done. Decorate with whipped cream and glacé cherries.

SWEET ROSEMARY SLICES

When Alison Ticehurst asked Dawn Carvey to make cakes for the Helmsley Walled Garden Café, she precipitated a career change for Dawn from banking to baking. This is one of the original recipes created by Dawn with help from her mother, Jean Gill, for the Café.

2 large eggs
150g (5oz) soft brown sugar
1 tsp vanilla extract
75g (3oz) melted butter, cooled
150g (5oz) plain flour
1 level tsp baking powder
2 tsp rosemary, chopped – fresh or dried
150g (5oz) dried fruit (sultanas, raisins, currants)
50g (2oz) glacé cherries in different colours if
   possible – or any other chopped glazed fruit you may have
75g (3oz) nuts, such as hazelnuts, almonds,
   brazils, walnuts or pecans — peanuts are not suitable
   because of their strong flavour

Line a 12,5 cm x 22,5 cm (5" x 9") tray bake tin with baking paper. Sift flour and baking powder together and set aside.

Scald the dried fruit in a colander and allow to cool. Place in a large bowl with the nuts, glazed cherries and the chopped rosemary. If using dried rosemary, chop finely and scald with a small amount of water to soften. Then add the rosemary and the scalding water to the mixture. Mix thoroughly.

Melt the butter in a small pan or microwave and allow to cool.

In a large basin, whisk the eggs, sugar and vanilla together until pale and thick. Gradually drizzle the melted butter into the mixture, whisking continuously. With a metal spoon, fold in the flour. Then mix in the fruit and nut mixture. Pour the mixture into the tin, level with the back of a spoon and bake immediately in a moderate oven at 170-180°C/325-350°F/gas mark 4 for about 35-40 minutes, until a skewer comes out clean. Reduce the oven temperature if the browning occurs too quickly.

Cut into square oblongs or triangles. Keeps for up to month in a cool place.

RICH APRICOT FINGERS

MAKES 18 SLICES

Lorna Fawcett, the garden designer, has provided this useful recipe for the occasional coffee morning, tea party or charity function, which makes sinfully rich and moist 'fingers'.

**150g (5oz) dried apricots, blended for 15 seconds
with 50ml (2floz) boiling water and set aside**

For the base:
50g (2oz) butter
125g (4oz) plain flour, sieved
25g (1oz) granulated sugar

For the topping:
40g (1½oz) self-raising flour, sieved
pinch of salt
50g (2oz) walnuts
175g (6oz) soft brown sugar
2 eggs
½ tsp vanilla extract
1-2tbsp icing sugar

For the base, rub fat and flour together to resemble breadcrumbs. Stir in the sugar and pack into bottom of a greased 20cm (8") square tin. Bake at 170°C/325°F/ gas mark 3 for 25 minutes.

For the topping, chop the nuts in a blender by dropping them through the hole in the lid. Switch off and add the brown sugar, vanilla, apricots and eggs. Blend for further 20 seconds. Pour into a bowl with the self-raising flour and mix thoroughly. Spread the mixture over the baked layer and bake for further 25 minutes at 170°C/325°F/gas mark 3. Allow to cool, sprinkle with icing sugar and cut into 'fingers'.

CRANBERRY MUFFIN CAKES

Also from the Ticehurst collection.

275g (10oz) plain flour
75g (3oz) castor sugar
1 tsp baking powder
½ tsp salt
½ tsp ground cinnamon
2 eggs, beaten
175ml (6floz) milk
125g (4oz) butter, melted
275g (10oz) cranberries, fresh or dried

For the topping:
75g (3oz) demerara sugar
75g (3oz) self-raising flour
50g (2oz) desiccated coconut
25g (1oz) butter at room temperature

Sift the dry ingredients together and repeat the process. In a bowl, mix eggs, sugar and milk and then add the melted butter. Sift the dry ingredients into this liquid mixture stirring as little as possible. Ignore lumps and do not over-mix. Fold in the cranberries. Distribute the dough onto a greased muffin tray.

For the topping, make a crumble by rubbing the fat into the dry ingredients. Mix well and sprinkle over the top of the cakes. Bake in a preheated oven at 190°C/375°F/gas mark 5 for one hour.

THE
HELMSLEY
WALLED GARDEN

DREAM CAKES

Alison Ticehurst had a dream: to save the Walled Garden from dereliction and to see it resurrected in its former glory. Apart from having learnt how to garden at her father's knee, she had little more than her own two hands and unwavering determination to achieve her aim. She was capable of inspiring her family, her friends and endless volunteers from all over who helped her to tackle the mammoth task of putting the Garden right. She was aware that some of her friends considered her as 'barmy' but this did not deter her from the stubborn pursuit of her dream and today's reality proves her right. Her dream cakes, too, are an inspiration.

For the crust:
225g (8oz) butter
450g (16oz) plain flour
4 tbsp icing sugar
pinch of salt

For the topping:
4 eggs
125g (4oz) sifted flour
500g (1lb) castor
pinch of salt
2 tsp baking powder
2 tsp vanilla essence
175g (6oz) walnuts, chopped
125g (4oz) candied cherries, chopped
125g (4oz) desiccated coconut

For the crust, rub fat into dry ingredients until the mixture resembles breadcrumbs. Spread evenly in a swiss roll tin and press down lightly with your fingers. Bake in a moderate oven for 5 minutes.

For the topping, beat eggs and sugar together until soft peaks form. Stir in the other ingredients and pour the mixture on top of the crust. Bake in a slow oven (150°C/300°F/gas mark2) for about thirty minutes, until the meringue topping turns light golden. Let cool and cut into squares with a sharp knife.

COLIN'S FLAPJACKS

Jean Gill, who together with her daughter Dawn was an early purveyor of bakeries to the Walled Garden Café, has let us have this recipe by her husband Colin. His flapjacks were a great success with his customers.

100g (4oz) margarine
4 tbsp golden syrup
75g (3oz) soft brown sugar
225g (8oz) rolled oats
75g (3oz) walnuts, chopped
rind of 1 orange, grated
½ tsp salt

Put margarine, golden syrup and sugar into a large pan. Melt all ingredients gently. Then add salt, rolled oats, orange rind and walnuts. Pour the mixture into a well greased 17,5cm x 30cm (7"x12") baking tin and bake at 170°C/325°F/gas mark 3 near the top of the oven until light brown. Let cool slightly; then cut into squares which should be removed from the tray before they cool completely.

CHOCOLATE BROWNIES

In Alison Ticehurst's collection, there is also a classic recipe for brownies.

175g (6oz) walnuts, chopped
125g (4oz) chocolate
175g (6oz) margarine
125g (4oz) sugar
2 eggs, beaten
225g (8oz) flour
1½ tsp baking powder
pinch of salt
a little milk

Melt the chocolate in a basin over hot water. Cream fat and sugar till soft. Add the beaten eggs and then flour, baking powder, salt, nuts and melted chocolate. Stir in a little milk to give the dough a soft consistency. Spread the mixture into a greased tin and bake in a moderate oven (180°C/350°F/gas mark4) for half an hour. Cut into squares while still warm and leave to cool.

CHEESE SCONES

MAKES 12-15

All Saints Church just behind the Market Place together with the ruins of Helmsley Castle dominates all distant views of Helmsley. A nineteenth century building erected in the thirteenth century style, it incorporates older features, some going back to Norman times. The vicar of Helmsley, the Rev. David Wilbourne, and his wife have contributed this recipe for cheese scones with a zip.

225g (8oz) self-raising flour
½ tsp salt
½ tsp dry mustard
25g (1oz) butter
100g (4oz) cheese, finely grated
150ml (½pt) milk

Preheat the oven to 220°C/425°F/gas mark 7. Sift flour, salt and mustard together. Rub in butter until mixture resembles fine breadcrumbs. Add all but one talblespoon of cheese. Bind together with the milk to form a soft dough. Roll or press out on a floured surface to a thickness of 1 cm (½"). Cut into rounds using a 4cm (1½") or 5cm (2") cutter. Place on a greased baking sheet. Brush with milk and sprinkle remaining grated cheese on top. Bake in a hot oven for 10-12 minutes. Cool on wire tray. Serve with butter.

WALNUT BREAD

Neil Booth, a member of the board of trustees of the Walled Garden, makes a rich walnut bread considered by his wife, Dorothy, to be his ultimate culinary achievement. It is especially good as an accompaniment for cheeses, particularly the blue Yorkshire varieties. He makes his bread with organic, stoneground, wholemeal flour, sometimes adding some malted flour containing cracked wheat, or some strong white flour for a lighter texture. But you could also use any of the pre-packed bread mixes, if you wish. Neil thinks a good walnut bread should be more like walnuts held together by dough than like a dough with a few walnuts lurking about the corners. A 350g/12oz lump of dough would then require at least 90g/3oz of nuts, baked gently beforehand in the oven. Since walnut bread is not a bread for every meal, small loaves are best. One kilo of flour makes four small loaves. A good option if you don't want to make bread regularly.

1 kilo (2lbs) organic, stoneground, wholemeal flour
30g (1oz) fresh yeast, available at any supermarket bakery department
600ml (a bit more than 1 pint) of tepid water
1 heaped tsp salt
60g (2oz) butter or margarine
1 tsp treacle
400g (14oz) walnuts, ⅔ roughly and ⅓ finely chopped and baked on a tray in the oven at 150°C/300°F/gas mark2 for 10 minutes

Dissolve yeast and treacle in the tepid water. Sift flour and salt together and rub the fat into this mixture. Stir in the liquid and knead for at least 5 minutes. Cover with a damp cloth and set in a warm place to rise until it has at least doubled in size. The time this takes is variable depending on temperature and other factors, typically from 1 to 3 hours. But don't worry too much, it really doesn't matter if the dough rises more than necessary. It should be on the moist side to make it easier to work the nuts in.

It is a bit of a battle to work the baked nuts into the dough. To achieve this, flatten the dough and pour the nuts into the centre. Fold up the dough over the nuts and start kneading. The nuts will do their best to escape, so keep pushing them back in until at last they give up the attempt. Shape your loaves and lay them on an oiled baking sheet or into a small oiled bread tin. Keep them covered and warm until they are adequately risen, which should take between 30 and 60 minutes. Laden with nuts, they will not rise quite as high as a plain loaf, and will continue to rise a little after they go into a hot oven. Bake at 210°C/410°F/gas mark 6½ for about 35 minutes, reducing the heat to 180°C/350°F/gas mark 4 after the first 15 minutes. When done, a tinned loaf should fall out of the tin when turned upside down and sound hollow when tapped on the bottom. Let the bread cool on a rack.

PINK PEPPERCORN BREAD

The recipe for this fragrant bread comes from the Appletree Inn in Marton. It makes a good accompaniment to many meals.

1¾ kilos (4lb) strong plain flour
45g (1½ oz) dried yeast or 21g (¾oz) fast action yeast
2 tsp sugar
4 tsp salt
2 tsp olive oil
2 handfuls of pink peppercorns
warm water

Mix all dry ingredients together, add the oil and lastly enough water to form a sticky dough. Knead well for at least 10 minutes. Then put in a clean container with space enough for the dough to prove and double in size. To achieve this, cover with a tea towel or cling film. It takes about an hour or two to prove, depending on the warmth of the kitchen.

The next stage is to knock the mixture back, i.e. to deflate it by a little kneading, and to cut it into desired shapes or to pack it into loaf tins, allowing of course for the dough to rise. Allow to prove again, then bake in a moderate oven for about 20 minutes or until you can feel or hear a hollowness when you lightly tap the bread underneath.

Egg-washing the dough will give a nice glaze finish. You can also dust the bread after baking for an alternative effect. Or try brushing it with melted butter and sprinkling it with seeds, such as poppy seed.

INDEX INDEX INDEX

NOTES